Fantasy Football Tips

201 ways to win through player rankings, cheat sheets and better drafting

By Sam Hendricks

Extra Point Press

Lynchburg Virginia

United States

www.XPPress.com

LIBRARY OF CONGRESS CONTROL NUMBER: 2009903375

ISBN: 978-0-9824286-6-5

Copyright © 2009 by Sam Hendricks

All rights reserved

Editing: Trish Hendricks

Foreword Edited by Eric Balkman

Printed in the United States of America by Lightning Source

Bulk purchases, please contact info@FFGuidebook.com

Additional Books by Sam Hendricks

Fantasy Football Guidebook: Your Comprehensive Guide to Playing Fantasy Football

-Named one of Top 4 Fantasy Football books of All-Time by RotoNation.com

-Award-winning finalist in the Sports category of the National Best Books 2008 Awards, sponsored by USA Book News.

-Finalist in the Sports category of the 2009 National Indie Excellence Awards.

Fantasy Football Almanac: The Essential Fantasy Football Reference Guide

Fantasy Football Almanac came about after Fantasy Football Diehards magazine asked Sam to be a member of their 2007 experts poll. He participated in the poll and mock experts draft. He decided to pass along his other 2007 insights and rankings in a book format that will appear again in future years.

The Almanac is unique in that Sam gives rankings based on different scoring systems and roster requirements. Scoring includes TD only, performance and performance plus formats. Leagues with two WRs and those with three WRs are also provided in addition to auction values and IDP rankings. Almanac also addresses keeper/dynasty leagues.

Fantasy Football Almanac 2008
Fantasy Football Almanac 2009

A soon to be released book on Personal Finance (May 2010)

Media Coverage

Look for Sam's expert advice and rankings in Fantasy Football Index, Fantasy Football Draftbook and other fantasy football magazines.

Sam also participates in a weekly "Ask the Expert" column at www.FantasyIndex.com

www.FantasyFootballGuidebook.blogspot.com where Sam blogs throughout the year.

Acknowledgements

A big hug and special thanks to my publicist, editor and communication specialist, Trish Hendricks, without her support and assistance none of my books would be as coherent as they have been in these two short years. My mother, Fannie also gets my biggest thanks since she always encouraged me to reach for new heights. I do not know if she envisioned fantasy football books back in those days of growing up on Wilson Avenue and then Berger Street, but she always had a smile and love that cheers me up even to this day.

To my lovely wife Birgitte, I owe everything. She completes me. Her understanding of late nights watching football and even longer nights drafting in high stakes leagues thousands of miles (and seven time zones away) constantly amazes me. But I fear our turf wars over the family computer have just started as she introduces the world to SewDanish, her Scandinavian Textile Art company which can be found at www.SewDanish.etsy.com and her blog at www.SewDanish.blogspot.com. Let the battle begin.

Thank you to Bill "Snigs" Singletary, a former aviator with me in the 336th Fighter Squadron at Seymour Johnson AFB. We flew F15-Es there. Snigs introduced me to this mistress called fantasy football.

An appreciative nod to my colleagues at work, who put up with my requests for no football talk on the Tuesday after Monday Night Football (if I have not seen the game yet). Sammy, Smurf, Tuna and Duck - your patience is a gift.

Finally to my diehard brothers in arms who play this great game of fantasy football with me: Bobby Floyd, Ned "Neckless" Rudd, Gary "Cowboy" Snyder and John "Kuz" Kuczka. Each of these gentlemen is like a brother to me and I would do almost anything for them (except trade them my stud RB).

I know I have left someone off who means much to me as well. This is for them. Thanks!

Foreword by David Gerczak
High Stakes Fantasy Player - Leroy's Aces
Co-Founder of The Fantasy Football Players Championship

My name is Dave Gerczak, but I go by the name Leroy's Aces in the fantasy football community. I can take this foreword in many different directions, but I've decided to do it from a somewhat unique perspective: From the point of view of a high stakes fantasy player.

To give you my background, I have played high stakes fantasy football since the creation of the World Championship of Fantasy Football (WCOFF) in 2002. I have enjoyed a significant amount of fantasy football success, too. I have earned two top-10 WCOFF finishes (out of 550+ players), 39th place overall in 2005, and I won the 2006 WCOFF Hall of Fame 24-team league. Before 2008, I had come close, but I had never won a national contest in those six years and—being a realist—never expected to win one either. Everything has to break right to actually win one, and the odds are deeply stacked against you.

But, 2008 was a year to remember for me. Two major fantasy football-related events transpired over the course of the year to considerably alter my life in the game.

In March of 2008, two other high stakes fantasy players, Lou Tranquilli and Alex Kaganovsky and I made a decision: We decided to launch a high stakes fantasy football contest. We felt that we could do a better job than some of the current industry offerings, which included a certain other contest that had defaulted on paying its prizes. In fact, Lou and Alex lost $16,000 in prize winnings because of these unfortunate circumstances. We were outraged and decided to form a contest that flipped the script on a traditional fantasy contest. We decided to call it the Fantasy Football *Players* Championship. (myFFPC.com)

Instead of focusing on building the contest and then advertising to get customers, we decided to build a contest on precisely what fantasy players wanted: A first (and still only) ever prize pool held in attorney escrow for the ultimate in player protection. Since the birth of our event, yet another high stakes contest has defaulted on paying prizes, so the attorney escrow has proven to be invaluable in protecting our players' interests. We added player-friendly rules, like a second "flex" player, additional tight end scoring and automated Elias Sports Bureau stat correction. We promised fat payout percentages and fast payouts and delivered on both of those promises. We issued a $75,000 grand prize along with offering a live/online hybrid draft format, and held our live draft in Caesars Palace. Our event drew 180 players, including Sam Hendricks, who played online and finished in a very impressive seventh place.

Many high stakes players applauded our rules, the attorney escrow, and the quick payouts. Chad Schroeder—team name Cocktails & Dreams—won our inaugural 2008 Main Event. While only a year old, the FFPC has already been a hit with high stakes players. We look forward to many more exciting and rewarding years, as we grow the concept as well as our community of players.

Forming and running the FFPC is a thrill and I love being a part of it. However, I must admit that the excitement of running that contest was temporarily surpassed by my fantasy teams' performance in the NFFC/NBC events. As one of its co-owners, I cannot play in the FFPC, so I decided to play in the National Fantasy Football Championship. My fantasy drafting partners, Kurt Awe, Eric Balkman[1] and I purchased three NFFC Main

---

[1] I generally will partner with friends Kurt Awe, Leroy Corson and Eric Balkman in NFFC and WCOFF fantasy drafts. I like to buy teams with friends as it is more fun to do so, and fantasy football is still all about having fun to me, no matter the cost. Sadly, Leroy was not part of the NFFC group…ouch.

Event teams—one in the NFFC Classic, and two in the NFFC Primetime.

The NFFC drafts were held in Chicago on a Saturday morning (Classic) and evening (Primetime), so Kurt and I drove down from Northeast Wisconsin on Friday afternoon. We met up with fantasy friends, Scott Atkins aka Team Legacy, and his buddy Mike Trent for a late dinner. Scott and Mike are excellent high stakes fantasy players and host the Red vs. Blue Show on BlogTalkRadio.com.

The next morning, Kurt and I drafted the NFFC Classic team together. The morning draft went well, as we snagged guys like Brandon Jacobs, Kurt Warner, Kevin Walter and Owen Daniels that we had pegged as good values going into the draft. The Primetime draft was a whole different animal—and a lot of fun—as Kurt and I each had to draft our own team. Seated about 100 feet away from each other, our drafts commenced at the same time. So, being the nosy person I am, every few minutes I would run over to Kurt and we would discuss the pick he was about to make. Then, I would cruise back over to my table and make my selection, occasionally snagging a cookie off the buffet table on the way. Truthfully, he didn't need me at all (and I didn't need the cookies), and after about eight rounds, I ended my in-between-pick jaunts.

Looking back, I do remember I felt really good about the prospects of both Primetime teams after the drafts. Kurt got loads of impact running backs and wide receivers, headlined by Chris Johnson and Antonio Bryant. Examining his roster, I noticed he did not draft a quarterback or tight end until the 11th round, for which I immediately ripped him. It was a little late for my tastes, but I figured we could snag a quarterback on waivers later, which we did with Matt Cassel.

The Primetime team he drafted ended up taking third in his 12-team league, but then got very hot in Weeks 14-16 (Kurt's team earned the top score Week 16 with 194 points). Kurt's Primetime team ended up winning the NBC Consolation Bracket, which grossed us $2,500. Waiver guys like Matt Cassel and Visanthe Schiancoe became late impact players for that team's playoff run. In fact, if Kurt's team had made the Championship round, it would have placed second overall out of 252 teams.

The team that we entered in the NFFC Classic contest did very well, also. It won the 14-team league for $5,000 by virtue of having both the best record and most points and ended up placing tenth overall out of 308 teams, just 29 points out of first place and $100,000.

Our other NFFC Primetime team won its league for $5,000, and moved onto the Championship weeks. In the first playoff week, we put up our best score of the season! Our team scored 198 points and took the early lead for the overall $100,000 title. In the NFFC, second place drops to $15,000, so it would have been a huge drop-off to finish below first. Week 15 offered us good matchups, and our team was able to notch 155 points in a relatively low-scoring fantasy week. Again, our team was somehow holding on as the highest scoring in the Championship bracket after week 15, and we had a pretty juicy 35-point lead over second place heading into the final week. I was a nervous wreck that week, as it was very stressful having a big lead.   I did not want to be the guy whose team choked in the fantasy playoffs or who started the wrong player which would cost us $85,000.

Our toughest Week 16 decision was whether to start Kurt Warner, who had little to play for at New England, or Phillip Rivers in a tough road game at Tampa. We originally had planned to start Warner, but the weather kept getting worse and worse in New England.   About an hour before the game, we heard reports of 60 mile an hour wind gusts headed to Foxboro, and at that point the decision was made to send Warner to the bench. Almost every fantasy ranking service had Warner ahead of Rivers, but we made our decision based on what we thought was right. That week, Kurt Warner managed only 30 passing yards before being benched, while Rivers threw for 287 yards and four touchdowns. In fact, Rivers had two touchdowns before Kurt even arrived to my house to watch NFL Sunday Ticket. Then, Steven Jackson scored, Tony Gonzalez scored, Isaac Bruce scored, and Brandon Marshall had another huge game. That night, Steve Smith scored once and DeAngelo Williams scored an incredible four times—it was a magical day! And that's how we won the NBC Primetime event for $100,000.

Due in part to the above mentioned players, our team exploded again for 184 fantasy points in Week 16, too. Leroy's Aces was in fact the highest scoring championship bracket team each week during the three weeks of the playoffs. We ended up winning the bracket by an astonishing 83 points over the second place team. And due to our strong NFFC Classic finish, our combined Classic/Primetime teams were the highest scoring combo of the entire tournament. That earned us free NFFC Main Event entries for 2009. Now that was one hell of a fantasy season, and it was all because of Sam's book!

OK—not really. But the concepts in Sam's first book did contribute to the base of knowledge I was able to bring into that draft and helped me walk away with $115,600 just over four months later.

Allow me to be completely honest. It felt amazing to win that event. To have your team play well all season and blow up during the playoffs is a wonderful payoff. It makes all of the player study and drafting effort I have put into this hobby worthwhile. It provides vindication. So when people ask me what I do as a hobby or what it is I am passionate about, I proudly tell them I play fantasy football.

"Really? You're a fantasy nerd?" I have heard that statement many times. And I laugh at it now. 35 million people.

That is how many fantasy nerds are actively playing just fantasy football. From 10-year-olds to grandmothers, from free Yahoo leagues to the $5,000 entry fee leagues like the FFPC Big Payback, it seems like everyone is playing fantasy football these days. The major networks like ESPN and CBS show scrolling stats all Sunday long to keep fantasy players happy. The fantasy football player base has gotten huge. It isn't just "nerds" playing fantasy football anymore. Fantasy football has gone mainstream.

But have the players gotten better? I don't think so. If anything, I think that the top fantasy players have gotten better, while the rest of the fantasy world is mired in mediocrity. I feel that fantasy football is very similar to no-limit Texas Hold 'Em, in that it takes a minute to learn, but a lifetime to master.

If you are reading this book, you are obviously willing to learn. Not many guys (or gals) will buy a book on this hobby. Maybe the latest magazines with some dated rankings, but a book? I am guessing that if you are reading this book, you do not simply play the free leagues, and you have already had some level of success in fantasy. In truth, the entry fee or level of competition doesn't really matter. What matters is that we, as players, are constantly striving to improve our fantasy skills. The difference between winning and losing in both the NFL and fantasy football has to do with attitude and effort. Of course, talent can't be taught, but it is amazing what hard work and a willingness to learn will do for you in fantasy football. You can be a head-case like Ryan Leaf or be a student of the game like Peyton Manning. And I think we all want to be known as the Peyton Manning of whatever fantasy football world we play in.

So how do you get better? Where do you go to tap the minds of the best fantasy footballers, and learn their deepest, darkest, and most profitable secrets? You need only to look and learn from one group: The high stakes players. They really are the best of the best. These people pony up their hard-earned cash, paying $1,000 or more per team to compete on the highest level of fantasy football. Sam Hendricks has one of those "elite of the elites" fantasy football minds.

I first met Sam in 2006, as we competed in a WCOFF Auction league. But the first time we actually spent any time together was in 2007. It was the day before the World Championship of Fantasy Football live draft in Las Vegas. He had just published The Fantasy Football Guidebook, and I came across his booth. After he finished with a few other players, I picked up a copy and talked with Sam for about 15 minutes. After speaking with him, I realized just how good the high stakes players are, as he was a wealth of knowledge. I spent most of the rest of the day reading his book, trying to glean some last minute tips prior to the main event draft. I could have easily blown off his book if I thought I knew better than some silly fantasy book. Instead, I blew off my friends for a few hours and went back to my room to read and learn. But as a high stakes fantasy player, I know there is always something more to learn, another way to look at things, and another perspective to consider. The Fantasy Football Guidebook was an excellent read and really covered all of the bases from beginner to advanced levels.

Sam, like me, played in the WCOFF for many years and was a player in the inaugural FFPC Main Event in 2008. If you have never played high stakes fantasy football, both Sam and I will attest that it is second to none. The competition is top-notch, the contests are run well, and it is truly a fun experience. I have met many, many friends over the years. They are all great people, and I meet more each and every year. It is never too late to join us and get in on the fun. (Players can enter for as little as $150 in a Satellite League.) So, whether you play the FFPC or one of the other high stakes events, I encourage you to take a leap and just play! You will not regret it.

Now, do I feel content with my fantasy skills after my big win in 2008? Hell, no! And neither should you, no matter how many championships you may have under your belt.   The fact that you are reading a fantasy football book already places you in rarified company. Having read all of these 201 tips, I can tell you I have learned many things and affirmed others. Some are common sense, but many are advanced concepts and have never before been revealed in print. What I love about a book like this is it can be reviewed at any time and any point of the book is a great starting point. I know it will be an annual refresher for me as I prepare for fantasy seasons in years to come. While I do not agree with everything Sam writes (i.e. the value of 3RR) he does share a lot of good fantasy wisdom on many levels.

In the book <u>Outliers</u>, author Malcolm Gladwell observes that the most accomplished people in each particular industry took about 10,000 hours to master their given craft. Whether it was Bill Gates, The Beatles, or Mozart, it takes roughly 10,000 hours or the equivalent of 5 years of full time effort to truly master a craft. Can fantasy football ever truly be mastered? I don't know yet, and neither does Sam. But we are both putting the hours in, and the best players in your leagues are, too. Are *you*?

Table of Contents

Chapter 1 Introduction

Why did I write another book on fantasy football? Let's face it, my first book, *Fantasy Football Guidebook: Your Comprehensive Guide to Playing Fantasy Football,* has done quite well (more than 1,000 copies sold to date) and my annual *Fantasy Football Almanac* has seen increased sales every year. So why do anymore? I should just sit back and relax and play fantasy football and enjoy my success.

But many have asked for **MY** advice on how to play and win at fantasy football. Comments like "Fantasy Football Guidebook is great and very comprehensive (400 pages) but we want to know which strategies YOU use. How do you calculate your rankings? Which tactics do use in the World Championship of Fantasy Football (WCOFF) or Fantasy Football Players Championship?

So I have written this book as a simple, straight-forward "guide" to my way of winning at fantasy football. So if you want the techniques and strategies that work the best from Fantasy Football Guidebook, this is your manual. *Fantasy Football Tips: 201 Ways to Win Through Player Rankings, Cheat Sheets and Better Drafting* is essentially "The Best of Fantasy Football Guidebook".

Good luck, and as always, drop me a line or a question at info@FFGuidebook.com league but gets no points even though he rushes for 150 yards but has no TDs? Or the owner who picked Mike Sellers in round 20 and only started him because he was in a jam with bye weeks? The bottom line is do not play in these leagues where picking the starting RB for a team gets you little or no points.

There are other scoring systems which favor luck more than skill, such as leagues with "bonus" scoring systems. In these leagues, players are awarded bonus points (usually 3 more points, so a 50% bonus) for TDs over a certain length (usually 40 or more yards). Again, how skilled do you have to be to figure out who will break several tackles this year and score long TDs? There is way too much luck involved in this type of scoring. Yes, you can predict that certain players will have a chance at longer TDs. Randy Moss and Tom Brady would be the perfect combo in this category. However, generally speaking, those who score that bonus are lucky, in that a defender fell down or missed the coverage.

Another league to avoid is the one where you draft a Head Coach and you get points for wins. Yes, there is some level of skill there, but come on …do you really watch games scouting head coaches and their potential to win a game?

This should lead to your next question. Then what leagues should I play in? Great question. Look for leagues that rely on performance scoring. 1 point per 10 yards rushing or receiving and 1 point per every 20 or 25 yards passing is fair. I also like Point Per Reception (PPR) leagues. These leagues tend to balance out the WRs and TEs to some degree and since you are going to be very good at ranking these players, you want to take advantage of a measurable statistic.

Another quality I look for is a league where there is at least one flex player and preferably two flex players. Flex players are starters that can come from a variety of different positions. Typically, a flex player can be a RB, WR or TE. Flex players help better drafters and can eliminate some of the consequences of injuries. If you have a great draft and get four star WRs but can only start 2 of them, then your drafting advantage is negated. However, if you are in a league that allows 2 WRs and 2 flex players, now all four WRs can start for you. Similarly, if you are starting one of your 3 great RBs as a flex but one succumbs to injury now, then one of your WRs can start as the flex player.

Finally, I look for leagues that start 3 WRs. This is both a start 3 WR and one flex or a start 2 WR and two flex type of league. Again, I feel that I have an advantage when it comes to spotting talent at the big four positions (QB, RB, WR and TE), therefore I want every opportunity to start more of them, since I think I am better at spotting talent than everyone else.

One last note of caution on league complexity. Complex means what I have discussed above, but not too complex or luck creeps back in. A league that awards points on passes made over 10 yards on third down is complex, but not skillful, to you. Fantasy Football Open Championship (FFOC) is kind of like this. In this league they award no PPR points, bonuses for over 40 yard TDs and 1 point per 10 yards rushing/receiving (25 for passing yards).

4 Victory Points (VP) versus Head to Head (H2H) or Total Points (TP) Leagues

In a H2H league, you play each team in your league once (12 teams = 11 game seasons, 14 team leagues = 13 game seasons). In a Total Points league, you do not play head to head matchups but instead accumulate points throughout the season and the team with the most points wins the league. TP leagues have an advantage in that they play for 16 and sometimes 17 weeks with no playoffs. Why is this an advantage? Every week is critical to awarding a champion. If you play in a H2H league, the playoffs may occur in week 12 or week 14. So, you have a shorter period of time to make the playoffs. Luck plays more of a role in H2H leagues.

Another outcome of H2H is the "luck" factor in who you play and when you play them. For example, you may face the best team in the league when he has tons of players on a bye week; lucky you! Your rival may face the same rival a week later when all of the previous players are off their bye. The case can be made that scheduling affects the outcome in H2H leagues. The other knock against H2H is the "you won against the weakest team in the league, but failed to outscore everyone else" argument. Sometimes you do not score well, but win, because you play the worst scoring team in the league that week. On other occasions, you can score the second most points for the week but still lose, since you played the highest scoring team. Argh! Read further for the solution to these vexing problems.

Even more alarming is the trend in H2H leagues for teams that are out of the running to fold up and quit playing competitively. In week 10, two games away from the playoffs, one team may face the top team who will do his best to win, of course, and you may face the bottom dweller that gave up weeks ago and does not even replace his bye week players. Not a fair situation. Pundits will argue that "it all works out in the end" but I do not think so. Theoretically you could play every team when they were full up (had no significant byes) and you were weak and your rival could have the reverse occur. In the latter weeks of the season you could face the top teams and he could face the worst teams, all simply because of the "luck" of the schedule. A Total Points league eliminates the potential for a "scheduling" bias.

TP leagues eliminate the schedule factor of luck but, quite frankly, they are not as popular (or fun). We, as owners, would rather face a live opponent than just strive to score the most points each week. We want to trash talk, compare rosters and watch and root against our opponent's players. We want to play in a H2H league for the excitement, but with some way of compensating for the schedule. The answer is victory points.

With Victory Points, you award 2 VPs for a win and zero points for a loss **AND** VPs for how well you scored versus the field as a whole. If you score in the top third you get 2 more VPs. If you score in the middle third of the teams, you get 1 VP, and if you score in the bottom third for the week, you get 0 VPs. So, a team can earn either 4, 3, 2, 1 or 0 Victory Points per week. The standings are based on Victory Points, with total points scored as the next tie-breaker.

In a 12 team league
Each H2H Win = 2 Victory Points
Each H2H Loss = 0 Victory Points

The top 4 Scoring Teams for that week = 2 VPs
The middle 4 Scoring Teams for that week = 1 VPs
The bottom 4 Scoring Team for that week = 0 VPs

In the example above, if a team wins but scores the 2nd worst points, they get just 2 VPs for the win and nothing else. If a team loses, but scores the 2nd most points for the week, they would get 2 VPs based on being in the top third of the league in scoring. Both teams get the same points because of opposite reasons. One team won, but did so with a poor score, and the other team lost, but did so with a great scoring performance. The team that wins and scores points in the top third of his league gets 4 VPs. So VPs compensate for a tough loss and a cheap win. It also keeps teams in it till the end, since you can gain a lot of ground with a win and top points in the last week (4 VPs). Look for leagues with Victory Points. Few use it, but those that do provide a fairer evaluation in H2H leagues.

5 Pick the Auction League over the Traditional Draft

An auction draft is the closest you will ever come to a luck-free draft. Auctions eliminate the draft spot bias. In an auction format, every team starts with the same budget amount of imaginary dollars (usually either $100 or $200). A player is nominated and then all owners get to bid on that player. Whoever bids the most of their budget gets that player and then their budget is reduced by the amount they agreed to pay for him. Everyone has the same chance to get that first player. After that, your budget will determine how much money you have to bid on the remaining players. It is capitalism at its finest in a fantasy football system.

In traditional drafts, the draft spot has an influence on your chances of winning. GASP! Say it isn't so, Joe. Yes, that's right folks, there is a dirty little secret out there that most purveyors of pay fantasy football leagues (whether it is CBSSPORTSLINE or the World Championship of Fantasy Football (WCOFF)) do not want you to know. The higher the draft spot (#1 being the highest), the more advantage you have to win. Depending on how the draft is executed, the advantage can be as much as 8%. (See Third Round Reversal of Fortune - 12 Teams Posted 8/4 by Jeff Pasquino, Exclusive to Footballguys.com).

6 Pick a league with a long Regular season-

The longer the season, the better because the longer you compete, the less luck plays a pernicious role. Imagine a league that only had a four game regular season and then had a 12 game playoff for the four playoff teams. Teams that start fast will make the playoffs and teams that start slow are doomed to miss the playoffs in this format. Would you want to play in that league? Only if you felt lucky enough to win early; again I try to minimize luck. The longer the regular season, the longer you have for those deep sleeper picks to bear fruit. You are going to be better than all of the other owners at finding them, but you have to have time for them to make their move. By the same token, those backup RBs you are stockpiling (Tip # 62) will not payoff right away, but give them a 13 game season versus a 9 game season, and you will do better every time.

So, longer is better. What is too short? FFOC had a 9 game regular season in 2008. Nine games? Give me a break. WCOFF and Fantasy Football Players Championship (FFPC) run an 11

have their final practice? It gets even dumber when the season shifts to Thursday games. Do you really want to pick your Sunday players on Thursday night?

13 Make sure the Super Bowl is in week 16

Do not play in a league that has the Super Bowl in week 17. These formats provide the worst "luck' factor of all. In week 17, many NFL teams rest their star players or play them minimally to prevent injuries. If IND has secured home field advantage throughout the playoffs, why would Peyton Manning risk injury in the last week of the season? Why would you want to play in the fantasy football championship game when luck will determine which of your players actually play in the NFL that week?

14 More playoff teams is better than less playoff teams

The first step to winning is finding the league in which you have the highest chance of winning. If you had a choice between playing in a league where 4 teams made the playoffs or two teams made the playoffs, which would be better? All else being equal, the league where more teams make the playoffs increases your chances of being in the playoffs. There can be some other issues which make this a limiting factor, but I will address those in more detail later. In general, the more teams that advance, the better your chance of winning.

Now let's say that same 4 team playoff format is available in a 10 team league or a 12 team league or a 14 team league. Which is better? Well, in a 10 team league, you have a 40% chance of making the playoffs. In a 12 team league, 33% make the playoffs and in a 14 team league, 28.6%. Again, all else being equal, I would rather play in the 10 team league where I have a better chance of making the playoffs. So look for leagues with more playoff teams and less total teams.

15 Playoff formats-Try and avoid single elimination

Try and find a league that does not have a single elimination playoff format. Unfortunately most leagues still use this format. A double elimination format, or even better, 2 week playoff rounds are preferred. In these cases, the playoffs last for 2 weeks and the combined score over the two weeks is used to determine the winner. If a single elimination tournament is used, does it use carry over points? Carry over points usually involve the average of the regular season carrying over into the playoffs. So if your average was 140 for the season, you would start round 1 of the playoffs with 140 points. It rewards a team that has scored the most points throughout the regular season. The same type of "reward" can occur through the playoff seeding. Seeding occurs when the top teams face lower ranked opponents based on their final regular season standings. Sometimes the top scoring team gets an easier opponent. In these cases, carry over points "overcompensates" this team.

16 Look for the highest Return on Investment (ROI)

What about Return on Investment (ROI) and payouts? How much you make when you win is another contributing factor. Normally, add all of the costs to play (entrance fees, transaction costs, other fees) and this is your investment. In leagues where there are no other costs except an entrance fee, it is easy. If it costs $200 to play, then that is your investment. To determine a league's payout, multiply this investment by all of the # of owners. This is how to quantify the number of participants in the payout equation. If 12 teams play, the total investment from all the owners is $2400. Now add up all the prize winnings. Everything that you can gain from the league should be considered as a return. Payout is how much is paid out to the owners versus their cost to play. If a contest pays out more than it collects the payout will be over 100%. This usually only occurs when a contest is starting out (in order to gain customers). If first place is $1000 and 2nd place is $500 and third place is $200 and no other winnings are awarded, then you have a return of $1700. Your payout is $1700/$2400 = 70.8%. And that is not a very good return on your investment. FFPC has an 85% payout on their satellite leagues. That is one of the highest payouts I have seen in a national contest.

ROI is determined by how much you invest and how much you win (or can win). So payout is about how much the contest pays back to the owners and ROI is about how much you as an owner can win. If you invest $250 but can only win $1775 (1st place is $1525 and $250 more for most points during the regular season), then your ROI is 7.1. That is a good return. The key concept to remember is you cannot win every prize awarded. You simply cannot win first, second and third place. So ROI concentrates on what you can win versus what it costs you to play. The higher the ROI the better. Payout is about what the contest takes and what it gives back to the players. The higher the payout the better too, but ROI can decrease even with a high payout if the prize structure is more evenly distributed. If two contests are the same (teams, total prize amounts, entry fees, etc) but one has just a first place prize and the other spreads the winnings out among three teams, then the contest with the single winner will have a higher ROI (all else equal).

ROI is higher when only one prize is awarded. ROI decreases when more than one team gets a prize.

17 Decimals-You want them!

Look for leagues that award points for every yard, not just on some of the yardage. If a league awards 1 point for every 10 yards, that is different than awarding 1 point per every yard rushing. If only whole numbers are used (1 point for every 10 yards), then players rushing for 66 yards get six points, and the additional six yards (66-60=6) are lost. However, if decimals are used (.1 point for every 1 yard) then the same player who rushed for 66 yards gets 6.6 points. Every yard is accredited points. In this case, using decimals gives full credit and using whole numbers robs you of points from that player. In my opinion, every little bit helps. The argument can be made that this rule helps/hurts everyone. But does it really? If you use all of these tips and are drafting/starting a superior team, then you want to get all of the points you can. Using decimals gives you all the points possible and that makes your team stronger.

18 Negative values

Negative values occur when a player scores more negative points than positive points (i.e. a QB throws 5 INTs and no TDs while passing for just 90 yards). In this scenario, he loses 5 points for the interceptions (INT = -1 point) and gains only 4.5 points for the 90 yards (90/20= 4.5). His total points are negative .5. In some leagues negative values are not used for total points. Still others allow negative points. Choose the league that allows negative points. Your players are going to be good; your opponents' players are more likely to fail. You want the bad players to be penalized for their bad play and their owners punished for starting them. Leagues that do not allow negative points give bad owners an advantage. Do not play in leagues where bad owners are given any advantage.

19 TE vs no TE

Some leagues have TEs who start, other leagues do not have TEs as a position that starts, and still others use TEs but only as a flex position option. I prefer to play in leagues with TEs because that is just one more position that I can be better than someone else at ranking and roster management. I have come to favor leagues that allow them as a starter and as a flex option, because if I draft two TEs who turn out to be great (or if I add one through free agency that turns out to be special), then I like to have the extra benefit they provide.

Look for leagues where TEs get an additional premium for catches. There are few TEs that are guaranteed TD makers. Receiving yardage is a better predictor but the area where a good TE excels is catches. Leagues that award 1.5 or 2.0 points per reception elevate TEs in value and represent the best possible scenario. If your other owners ignore the TE position, so much the better. You can gain valuable ground on them by selecting TEs who can start as flex and will provide extra points over their TEs.

20 Complex starting lineups

Some leagues have simple starting lineups like one QB, RB, WR, K and Defense. Still others start one QB, 2 RBs, 2 WRs, TE, K and Defense. If a flex position is added the starting roster becomes more complex (1/2/2/1/1/1+1 flex position). Adding a third WR adds even more complexity as owners scramble for three serviceable WRs to start. The more complex leagues start multiple players from the RB and WR position and have multiple flex positions (1/2/2/1/1/1+2 flex positions). **Complex starting rosters favor advanced players.** The more options I have, the better chance I have of showcasing my skill as a footballer and beating my opponents. So, go with leagues that start multiple flex positions and multiple players at RB and WR, where your techniques at drafting can give you lots of great players. If faced with the dilemma of choosing between a league that starts 3 WRs and a flex or one that starts 2 WRs and 2 flex positions, pick the league with 2 flex positions. In this league you will have many more options (yes, so will your opponent) but thanks to Chapter 6 Roster Management, you will have more of an advantage.

21 Prize Distribution

Look for a league that awards prize money to the top three finishers, as opposed to paying all the winnings to the Champion team. This may sound like heresy since with the past tips (Tip #16) I have been preaching how well you will do if you use all of the tips in this book, and you will be the Champion. As hard as this is for me to say, luck still plays a pernicious part in fantasy football, no matter how well you prepare and what steps you take to remove it from the hobby. I say FF is 25 % draft preparation, 25% draft skill, 15% free agency acquisition skill, 20% starter/bench skill and 15% luck. Luck, in that you avoid injuries, suspensions, releases or other team issues or that your opponents have these misfortunes befall them. I hate to have my championship team fall in the League Championship game and then get absolutely nothing to show for a great season minus one game. There are too many variables when you play a H2H format to think you will win every time. Better to expect to make the playoffs every time and get something to show for every playoff team.

Weekly prizes for the highest scoring team are another way to spread some of the prize money around. I like this idea if the league is a total points league but not if it is a H2H league. In a total points league, I draft my team to score the most points over the season and thus should have a good chance to outscore more times than not, but in a H2H league consistency is a better option. Which team would you want in a H2H league? One that scores 1100 points in the 11 game season but does it with hot and cold players so that they score 160 points five times and 50 points for the remaining five games? Or a team that only scores 1000 points but averages 91 points per game? The higher scoring team finishes 6-5, as they won all their big scoring games, but dropped five of their six low scoring games. The other team finished 7-4 with their 91 point average beating many teams as the league average was 84. **Avoid weekly prizes unless you are drafting a total points team.**

22 Make sure the league pays out in a timely manner

This is more of a pet peeve of mine than a real warning, but it is a great feeling to win and an even better feeling to receive the winnings check shortly thereafter. Nothing puts a downer on the experience faster than winning in late December and not getting the check until February or later. There have been some instances of late checks in recent years and I think it is a case of companies raking in the interest on the prize money in order to make some extra profit. Lets face it, if I owed you $2,000, the longer I held on to it the more interest I can make from that money. Winners should be paid by the middle of January at the latest. Look for leagues that are a) upfront about the NLT date for when you will be paid and b) make that pay by date sooner rather than later.

23 Make sure league message board (MB) is active and fun

This should not be a showstopper as far as league choice is concerned, but an active message board where the players are good-natured, intelligent and fantasy-focused makes trash talking and general MB ranting more fun. The message board should be easy to use and easy to read. Normally you will hit it on the weekends before the games and the last thing you need is to have an eye exam or IQ test to be able to post.

24 Tiebreaker rules

How are the ties broken? Are they broken at all? Some leagues allow H2H games to be a tie in the standings. Still others go to some tiebreaker formula. Still others allow ties for regular season games but have a tiebreaker formula for making the playoffs or advancing in the playoffs. Try to find a league with the tiebreaker for advancing to the playoffs based on total points as opposed to H2H meetings. Just because a team wins in week 7 does not mean they are the better team (see Tip #4). A better measure of strength for tiebreakers is total points scored for the season.

25 Look for leagues that are weighted toward a position or positions you do well in evaluating

Do you find that your QB rankings each preseason tend to be very good yet your TE rankings…well, they stink? If so, look for leagues that emphasize QBs and perhaps that do not have any TEs. Look for leagues that start 2 QBs or that give 6 pts per TD passing and that have no TE or use a 3 WR or flex starters. Just remember two important things. QB is perhaps one of the easiest to predict. Why? Not a lot of QB by committee, or too many injuries to the position in general, and the position tends to be very consistent in the middle of the pack. When I say this I mean there is not too much difference between the 12th and 20th QB. So, if your rankings are a little off kilter, it probably is not a death knell. Mess up on the RBs or WRs and that is a different story altogether. Hopefully your rankings/predictions/projections of RBs and WRs are your greatest strength, because they will be a large focus in almost every league. But in case you are a poor judge of WR talent, consider playing to your strengths and not your weakness in this case. If WRs are just not your thing, then pick a league that de-emphasizes WRs. Some leagues only start 1 WR or only 2 WRs. Definitely stay away from starting 3 WRs and 2 Flex positions as they tend to see the most 4 and 5 WR lineups.

26 Draft date

Play in a league that drafts the closest to the start of the NFL regular season. Some leagues will have drafts that start as early as June (almost 4 months before the season starts in mid September). The closer you get to the start of the NFL season, the more accurate information you have on who will be the starters and who will ride the bench. All of the free agent acquisitions will have transpired and all of the injuries from preseason should be known. In essence, you will be more informed the later the draft occurs. Why is this all so important? To reduce the luck factor. There is nothing worse than drafting a RB in June as the starter and then he gets hurt in the preseason and is out for the season. If you drafted in June, that injury affects your team or that injury gives the unskilled owner a victory in the early part of the season that he should not have had. Any way luck can be reduced, favors the prepared.

If you draft in an early draft, you may have more insight into what a team plans to do or will do in the upcoming season, but the slight advantage you have is negated by the unlucky injuries, suspensions or trades that can and will occur between when you drafted and when the season starts.

27 Draft after the kickoff game on Thursday

You may have the choice of a draft some days before the season kicks off on Thursday, or one that actually drafts on the Saturday after the Thursday kickoff game but before the Sunday games in week 1. If so, again draft on the later date, so Saturday in this case. Why? You can take advantage of the biases that may develop from that Thursday game. Players that played on Thursday and did well will get a premium assigned to them on draft day. Likewise, those that performed poorly will lose some rankings on owner's draft sheets. You can take advantage of this. If you expect Reggie Wayne to be the #1 WR, yet he plays in the Thursday game and has only one catch for 12 yards, others will panic on him. Not you. You will be able to draft him in a later round perhaps and benefit from this discount. Another way to take advantage of this "known game" is if an unknown player "goes off". I remember one year Charlie Batch played in the game for Big Ben, who would return the next week. Batch's stats were great but would more than likely be his only ones for the year. Smart owners grabbed him with a late draft pick (one that would normally have been for a long sleeper) and played him in week 1 to get his fantasy points before dropping him the next week to get a sleeper.

28 Draft type

Some leagues will offer an option of drafting live with other owners or online or by phone. There is some debate about which is more advantageous. The first thing to consider is, are all the drafts at the same time? If one is at a different time, then use Tip # 26. If they are all at the same time, then choose the online option. The online option has the following advantages:

1) Comfort -You can draft in your pajamas if you want, with food and beverages nearby and your own bathroom.
2) You can have the most current information via your computer.
3) If you wished to include friends, they could be present to assist you in your draft. Phone a friend anyone?

Live drafts do present an opportunity to eyeball your opponents and maybe find a weakness (like if they are homers and will be picking a certain team's players predominantly).

29 If not Auction-serpentine, 3RR, Bonsai

If you cannot choose an auction format, but instead go with a traditional draft, the next question is: How is your draft spot determined and what is the draft order? Avoid straight line drafts, seek Third Round Reversal (3RR)(Tip # 131). Better yet try and find a Bonsai draft format, where the draft is reversed in the second, third and fourth rounds (Last team picks first in round 2, 3 and 4) and tries to even out the draft spot inequality then goes back to a serpentine method for the remaining rounds. This is the fairest of all.

Chapter 3 Rankings

As with all player rankings, start with last year's rankings. Do not worry about their statistics quite yet; just where they ranked numerically within their position. Delete any players who have retired or who are expected to miss the season due to injury. Add their replacements at the same rank to start. Then follow the tips below.

30 QB Rankings

Checklist

A) Put all of the starting QBs in your top 32. Put QBs who are competing for the same job on the same line separated by a slash with the favorite listed first (Ex Kurt Warner/Matt Leinart). Any QB who has competition for his job should be far down the rankings based on the unknown of who will start (i.e. not in your top 15). How far down? Definitely not ranked in your list of required QBs - if 12 teams and a start 1 QB league this would be top 12. Do not take chances with backups until the late rounds. A backup QB who may be a good QB if he starts can be drafted but only as a backup. Never draft a questionable starter as your #1. Taking such a chance is perfect if you have a solid #1 QB who has a late bye week. Now you have some time to see if your sleeper QB starts and pans out.

B) Look at past history. Is the QB consistent with his TD passes and yards? Do not forget those rushing TDs. Not many QBs get more than two rushing TDs a year and they are hard to predict. But the Tarvaris Jacksons and Aaron Rodgers should be expected to rush for more TDs, which may be worth more. Usually the younger the QB the more likely he is to rush for more than 2 TDs a year.

C) Look at his WRs. Did he gain or lose any quality WRs? This should be reflected in his ranking. If not, then expect the same stats and ranking.

D) Finally, look at his OL and Head coach. Does he have the same OL protection? Losing a blind side tackle to free agency or injury usually hampers QBs stats. Does he have a new head coach or a new offensive scheme? It may take a year to learn either.

31 RB Rankings

A) Make sure you start with all of the RBs from last year. If they were in a running back by committee (RBBC) but now are the main RB or vice versa, rank them appropriately. (i.e. raise them or lower them based on their situation this year). {RBBC occurs when two RBs split significant time and touches. One example may be a RB who is the goal line specialist, while the other is the everydown back (except near the goalline)}.

B) OL/Head Coach/Offensive Scheme - Did the team lose 2 of their 5 linemen? If so, lower the RB in the rankings. Did the team just get a great QB who can force the defenses to stop using eight man fronts? If so, raise him in your rankings. Did the team hire a new HC who is run oriented? If so, raise him up in those rankings.

C) Downgrade hurt RBs appropriately. If they had off-season surgery, hedge your bets - don't rank them too low, but don't bet the ranch on them either.

D) Look for RBs on well-balanced offenses (teams with QBs expected to pass for 3200+ yards and 20+ TDs - normally your top 12 QBs).

32 WR Rankings

A) Take the top two WRs from every team. This gives you 64 WRs. Now add in the WR3 from the teams that are expected to be passing machines this year. There are only a few teams that have 3 WRs in the top 40 in a year (AZ and IND in 2008). This should give you about 70 WRs. After you add in some rookies (about 10) and sleepers (another 10), you should have 90 WRs ranked. That is enough for seven WRs each in a 12-team league.

B) Rank players based on last year's stats to start. Then adjust (prorate) for injuries. Look at their past production. Reward consistency.

C) QB/HC/offensive scheme - Do they have a great QB throwing the ball? Is there a new philosophy? Will the WR get more touches or less this year?

D) Are they an end zone option? Look for tall WRs with great leaping ability (think Randy Moss or Larry Fitzgerald) or small speedsters (Steve Smith or Santana Moss).

33 TE Rankings

A) Start with last year's rankings, based on statistics.

B) QB/WR/OL/HC/offensive scheme changes - if a star WR leaves or is hurt then sometimes the TE gets the extra looks. On the other hand, if a OL is hurt or leaves many times the TE is forced to stay in and block, thus limiting his touches.

C) Look for second and third year TEs who are tall with great leaping ability (see WRs Tip #32). A dead giveaway is if they were former basketball players in college.

34 Do K Rankings last

Doing the kicker rankings last allows you to see how you expect the offense to perform and the defense as well (based on your rankings). Both are strong determinants for kicker performance. A good offense should score many points (FGs or XPs) and a good defense will give the offense more opportunities and better field position to score too.

35 K Rankings

A) Starting with last year's rankings, look at their FG percentage inside of 40 yards. Any kicker with two or more misses inside 40 will be on a short leash. Avoid them if possible unless they are in top 15. If they are not in the top 15, move them to the bottom 10. If your league penalizes you for missed FGs, look harder at their FG percentage. Most top 10 kickers have an 85% FG percentage but don't penalize for long FG misses (50+ yards).

B) If you are in a league that rewards longer FGs, look for how many were attempted beyond 40 or 50 yards.

C) Has the QB/HC/holder/long snapper or offensive scheme changed? If so, watch them carefully. Many times a change at any of these positions upsets the apple cart and the kicker drops in the rankings.

D) How did the team's defense do last year? Is it expected to improve? Bump up a few spots those kickers whose defense improves from last year due to free agency.

E) Remember that many of the top 5 kickers this year will come from the top 15 last year, so try to find those kickers that ranked 6-15th last year that might move up based on the above criteria. Look for kickers on top 10 scoring offenses or top 10 yardage offenses.

F) I give kickers in a dome a little nudge up the rankings since half their games are in a controlled environment.

36 DEF/ST Rankings

"Sacks and points/yardage allowed tend to be the most consistent statistics among defenses based on the talent on the field" -Fantasy Football Guidebook, so look for teams that consistently rank high in these categories. Look for teams with 40 or more sacks. Ignore safeties, turnovers and defensive TDs as these are hard to predict and fluctuate from year to year. Who you play and who the QB is for that team is highly correlated with how many turnovers a team will make.

A) Has the defensive coordinator or HC changed? Sometimes this can be for the good, other times for the bad. Is the new HC defensive minded? Are they changing to a new scheme (3-4 or 4-3)?

B) Look at who they have gained/lost due to FA, retirement, trades or injuries

C) Last year's top 5 defenses in terms of sacks, points and yardage allowed usually stay in the top 15. For the same reason, last season's terrible defenses in those same terms will not improve much, so expect them to stay in the bottom 15.

D) Some teams are good bets as a top defense, year in and year out. Make sure Pittsburgh, Miami, Dallas, Jacksonville, and Baltimore are all high on your rankings. Denver and Tampa Bay used to be in this category but recent coaching changes in both cities make me skeptical of giving them the same recognition now.

37 Individual Defensive Player (IDP) Rankings

Use Value Based Drafting (VBD)(Tip# 96) to determine when to start drafting IDP. But there are lots of IDP on the waiver wire, so do not forget to factor in supply and demand into VBD. Look for "bend but don't break" defenses, not great defenses. The great defenses (example BAL) force so many "three downs and a punt" scenarios that they do not get lots of chances for tackles and turnovers. NE, on the other hand, has a "bend but don't break" attitude and they stay on the field more often. On the field more means more chances for an IDP to score points. Another factor will be an offense that is not good, thus giving the ball back and putting their defense on the field again. In fact, having a great rush defense actually hurts the defense since that will force the other team to pass, in which case they usually move quickly or kick it away. Great defenses (especially great rush defenses) are a hindrance to great IDPs.

Forget the hype. The media loves to focus on the sack leaders but many times those guys are behind in fantasy points (FPs) because of they do not have many tackling opportunities. Know your FP projections and do not bite off on the big names but little IDP producers. (If your league does not require defensive linemen (DL) then go with linebackers (LBs) almost exclusively). The guy who tackles well is the one you want, not the one that show boats after a sack or INT and gets all the ESPN highlight time. Ignore the INT and fumbles recovered stat. They are hard to predict and there is not much difference between the leader and the #25 guy. Look at solo tackles; they are the bread and butter of IDP scoring. Some leagues allow 1 point for every 20 return yards. If so, note which DBs are return men since this is a nice chance for more points.

38 Use Average Draft Position (ADP) carefully

ADP, you either love it or hate it. ADP is a way to determine at what point a player is drafted in other drafts. ADP should present the highest pick and lowest draft pick used to add

a certain player and the average draft pick along with the
number of mock drafts sampled.

Two sample ADPs for Reggie Wayne are below:

Player Drafts	Pos	Team	ADP	High	Low	#
Reggie Wayne	WR	IND	2.3	1.10	3.01	50

Player Drafts	Pos	Team	ADP	High	Low	#
Reggie Wayne	WR	IND	15	10	25	50

In the first example, ADP is based on the number of teams
in the league (in this case 12 teams) and the round is given as a
whole number and the draft spot within that round in the number
after the decimal. Therefore, 2.3 is the 2nd round of the draft and
the third pick of that round.

In the second example the same information is presented
but the overall pick number is always given. So the same 2.3
above is actually the 15th overall pick. **Make sure the ADP data
you use is for the same scoring system, starting lineup and
number of teams as your league. Using data from leagues
other than your format can skew the data unfavorably.** Be
careful with overall ADP data as it can easily come from leagues
with the different numbers of teams than your league.

I think it is a wonderful tool to determine what others may
think of a player's worth. Use the ADP to determine which
players others undervalue (ADP is lower than your rankings) or
overvalue (ADP is higher than your overall ranking). Use the high
and low picks to determine your probable window of opportunity
for drafting a player. For example, if you like Player A and his
ADP is 5.01 (high 4.09, low 6.01) and you have the 9th pick in the
4th round (4.09) and the 4th pick in the fifth round (5.04), you
should draft him with your 4th pick (rather than wait) since he will

probably be drafted before your fifth pick comes around (his ADP says there is a good chance he will be drafted in the late 4th or early fifth round).

What is the source of the ADP data? Does it come from a blog with no known qualifications? Or does it come from a respected mock draft web site? Even if it is from the web site where thousands of mock drafts occur, is the ADP the right fit for your needs. Put another way, garbage in, garbage out. Make sure the data is for your league specifics (see Tip #39).

39 Make sure the ADP data is for the same type of league you are in (scoring rules, starters, # teams)

There is no reason to use ADP data if it is for drafts that have different rules than your league. If your league awards only 4 points per passing TD but the ADP is for leagues that award 6 points, than their ADP will have QBs drafted much higher than your league. Imagine how skewed the data will be if it is for leagues that start TEs but you do not have to start a TE. In this case you may not even have to draft a TE or only as a flex backup. Finally, what if the ADP data is for 14 team leagues and your league has 10 teams. Teams will draft positions differently based on the demand that is created by the number of teams playing (See Tip # 95 –Appendix B).

40 Make sure ADP is the latest (most current)

ADP data is only a snap shot in time. Make note of the day it was created and the time span the draft data includes. If you use ADP data from a week ago (time span was long), then it will have flaws if a major injury, trade or announcement occurred. If Matt Forte announces he injured his foot and will miss the season, the ADP for all Chicago Bears players will change significantly. In this case the ADP data is too old. Even if the data is created after the event, if it includes most drafts from before the event (in this case Forte's injury), the ADP data is useless. Best to have data created the day before the draft and with a short time horizon so as not to include drafts in the past that did not know about the most recent events.

ADP data can get old fast. If your ADP is from yesterday before the breaking news that a certain top QB broke his arm and is out for the season, then the QB , his WRs, TE and even the RB need to be adjusted because their ADP is going to fall based on the current news.

41 Make sure ADP comes from real drafts (where the owners had their own money on the line)

All too often the ADP data comes from mock drafts where "owners" (and I use the term loosely) can log on and draft and they have no "empowerment" or sense of ownership. If they participate in a mock draft , wanting to see what would happen if they drafted three WRs to start, this would mess up the results since no owner would use this strategy in most draft situations. I have seen owners draft kickers way too early or their entire favorite team's players (homers big time). Make sure the ADP data comes from real drafts where owners paid an entry fee. **The higher the entry fee the more serious the draft results.**

42 Do not follow ADP blindly; use it as a tool but not as the scripture from on high

ADP has many flaws as discussed in previous tips. If you follow those tips though, ADP can be a good predictor of when a player is drafted, on average. You can use this as a tool to beat others to the punch. But remember, not everyone is average. There may well be some "sharks" in your draft. They may even be reading this book right now. They will know to jump early if needed. So the numbers from ADP are just that, the average expected draft position, not a guarantee that every draft will fall that way.

43 Average Value Theory (AVT)

Use AVT by Wade Iuele to get the expected fantasy points for player rankings. AVT suggests that rather than calculating your own projections you should use the average value of players in that positions ranking for the last few years. Instead of beating your head against the wall trying to come up with projections for what every player is going to do statistically next year (how many TDs, yardage, catches etc), simply use what the average has been for that position's rank over the past three years. Let history be your guide. So rank your players within each position (see Tip #30-37) but then use the three-year average fantasy points for that position instead of your own projections.

For example, if you have player D ranked as your fourth WR (WR4), use the average fantasy points for the fourth best WR over the past 3 years, using your league's scoring system. In this case, 240 pts in 2006, 252 in 2007 and 254 in 2008; so 249 is the 3-year average. If you feel that a significant change occurred in one of the previous years, you could even weight them at a ratio of less than one to one. For example, 2006 and 2007 might only have a weighting of .9 or 10% less than the 2008, because they were before the rule change about "forced out".

Now you can add the expected total fantasy points for every position to your rankings. You will use these fantasy points to compare players in different positions to determine an overall ranking for use in the early rounds. But that will come later with VBD.

44 Use 3 Year AVT data

I use the three-year average because it gives a good capture of trends (two years is too short) but does not get too bogged down in old rules (five years or more).

45 Tiering

A little-used but significant process to minimize the "pucker factor on draft day" is tiering. Tiering or "bucketing", as it is also known, groups players of equal value on your cheat sheets. A tier is a group of players with about the same expected performance for the season in terms of fantasy points. You should feel that all of the players in a tier are about the same and should have no remorse about getting one of them versus some other player in the same tier.

Normally in the leagues you will be playing in (Chapter 2) a 15-20 point range will qualify as a tier (i.e. players within 20 fantasy points of each other can be expected to perform about the same). Look at your rankings for each position with player's names and their total expected fantasy points (from AVT Tip #43).

A) Subtract your tier point reference (20 points) from the top player in that position. Now all the other players after him that have fantasy points within that range should be in the same tier. The top RB according to AVT is expected to score 300 points. Subtract 20 points from 300 and now any player scoring between 280 and 300 is in the top tier. Draw a line in pencil under the last player in that group. Now repeat with the next player down your list who is outside the first tier. Subtract 20 points from his total and draw a line under the last player within that group.
Only tier for possible starters and one backup at each position. Once you get to beyond the backup, there is no need to delineate between scrubs.

B) When you are finished, look at who is where. You should believe that all players within a tier are the same. If not, move the players or the tier lines to get them in the same grouping.

C) Look at the number of tiers you have. You should have no more than four for QB, TE, K and Defense and maybe six for the more abundant RB and WR rankings. The QB, TE, K and

Defense positions will have a top or "Stud" tier that will be small (anywhere from 3-8 players), the "Good" tier will be the next with 7-12 players. After those 15 or so players, there is the "OK tier with another 10 players and then the remaining starters make up the last tier. Finally, any players starting but on shaky ground need to finish up the rankings outside the last tier.

Tiers do not have to all have the same number of players. Some tiers may be small (usually the top tier) and some may be large (the QB and WR positions have large groupings of similar players). Add discriminators (see Tip# 77) to help pick within tiers, if able.

46 Draft from higher tiers first (RB, WR primarily), draft from shallow tiers when the high tiers are depleted, and wait to draft from deep, lower tiers until the absolute last minute.

Fantasy Football Guidebook goes into more detail about tiering and the methods to use.

47 Consistency

Draft players who are consistent. Easier said than done. Matt Waldman's Consistency score (CRANK) is a good method of determining consistent players. He looks at their fantasy scores on a week-to-week basis and season-to-season basis. He looks for players who will score high fantasy points but will do it week in and week out, versus being more boom and bust. Much better to have player A that scores 15 points a week on his way to 240 total points then have a player B who scores the same 240 points but does it by scoring 35 points for five games and 5.9 points for the other 11 games. You are much more likely to get frustrated with the more frequent poor performance of player B and have him benched on a week when he explodes, thus losing the benefit of his great day. The same metaphor can be used to buying a small cap growth mutual fund or an index fund. You are more likely to be tempted to sell the small cap growth mutual fund when the market goes down because it is has higher losses than the index fund. Since you cannot time the stock market, better the buy and hold method of "steady Eddy wins the race".

48 Ignore the "Don't draft a Rookie" advice

Notice few mentions of rookies in previous tips. That is because, taken as a whole, they are not good. Most rookies will disappoint.

Any player drafted with one of the top five picks will play soon. RBs start quicker than any of the other positions (other than kicker) as it is an easier transition. QBs have to learn the offensive scheme, WRs and TEs need to learn the routes, all of which usually takes at least a year to get really good. RBs, on the other hand, just look for the holes to run through. Many rookie RBs will not be in on passing downs, as they have to learn who to block and when, so even if they do start they may not play as much as a veteran RB. For this reason RB rookies tend to be overvalued in their ADP (or spot on, but rarely undervalued). One exception to this rule was 2008 and Matt Forte, but again that is the exception rather than the rule.

A RB drafted in the first two rounds of the NFL draft can be ranked as a low end RB2. They probably will not start (unless a top 5 as mentioned above). Make sure that rookies with an opportunity are ranked high enough on your cheat sheet.

Rookie QBs rarely start and if they do the learning curve is quite high and expensive (too many INTs not enough TDs). Avoid them.

Rookie WRs drafted early in the NFL draft (1-3 rounds) have a 15% chance of becoming a fantasy starter (Top 35 WR). Of that group, only one of three will be Top 25 material. So, your chances of drafting a Top 25 rookie WR is about 1 in 20. Do not let that stop you from trying, though. If anything, WRs can be a gold mine that other owners do not explore. Too many owners have the "don't draft a rookie" mentality, and this lets you have an area where you can excel. Look for rookie WRs with opportunity and a good situation. Opportunity is obvious - were they drafted to replace a retired, traded or injured veteran? If so, he has a good opportunity to start. The situation depends on the offensive scheme of his team and who is throwing him the ball. Is the team a run first team with a low ranked QB? Or is it a pass happy offense with a gunslinger tossing the rock? Gamble on a rookie WR late in the draft instead of a bench warmer who may never start for you.

49 Character issues

Evaluate players based on previous off the field and on the field (in terms of Steve Smith slugging his teammate) issues. Lower the rankings of players who have a history of getting into trouble. Anything that reflects poorly on the NFL will be punished and result in suspensions. That means missed game time for your fantasy team unless it is week 17. Players who you have no reason to suspect will ever be problems now get a premium. It is a pretty safe bet that Peyton Manning will never be arrested at a strip club for shooting someone. He moves up in the overall rankings because some other idiot cannot stay out of trouble.

Most of the "bad boys" of the NFL are known. The rookies coming into the league are the unknown. Dig a little deeper if you like the situation a rookie RB or WR is in, do your due diligence before risking a draft pick on them.

50 Mock Drafts

Mock drafts are "practice" drafts where owners get to draft but the results of the draft do not count. After the draft, no league forms. Mock draft sites allow you to join an upcoming online draft and see how it goes with no retribution. Practice makes perfect and that is where mock drafts can be a great tool. Just make sure the starters and scoring rules are about the same. No reason to mock draft in a 10 team TD only league when you play in a 14 team PPR performance league.

Mock drafts are important for several reasons. First, they let you practice using your own strategy (see Chapter 4) while making time-critical decisions. Second, they let you see who is drafted and where; this helps you find trends, see how your rankings stack up and find deep sleepers that you may have overlooked. Third, you will see where the position runs occur. Position runs occur when majorities of owners start to draft players from the same position (TE runs in the fourth round are common). Finally, you can use your mock drafts as an unofficial ADP.

Here are a few things to keep in mind when doing mock drafts. Make sure everyone shows up, because one owner using an automated computer program to do his draft ruins the results. Additionally, make sure all the owners draft realistically. One owner drafting four TEs and three kickers skews the results as well. If you really want to know when a player will be selected - do not draft him and "let the market decide." Remember the results of a mock are best right after that draft and the older the results, the more they are influenced by other, more current events. If Player A becomes injured after your mock draft, he and others on his team will change in value.

51 Cheat sheets

Cheat sheets are simply your rankings, but with a few added bits. Cheat sheets should have players ranked by position and an overall ranking for the first 100-120 players. The overall ranking helps you draft for the first seven or eight rounds (the early part of the draft). Cheat sheets should consist of four pages: an overall ranking, QB/TE ranking, RB/WR ranking and a K/Defense ranking. Player's names, rank, position, bye week and ADP should be on each line (see Appendix C Cheat Sheets Sample-QB). Off to the right you should also have room for notes on injuries, team issues, suspensions, strength of schedule

(SOS) and asterisks for sleeper potential and an arrow for going up or down in value recently.

The cheat sheets should have your tiers on them as well (See Tip # 45). Sleepers can be highlighted in yellow to annotate where they are. Pete Smits in *Fantasy Football for Blood and Profit* suggests notations along side the cheat sheets (beside a player) such as "++" or "?" where the "magnitude of the arrows, question marks, etc. is used to assess approximate degree of each."

52 Don't toss those old cheat sheets

Do not throw away your cheat sheets after the draft. Instead, use it to evaluate dropped players (if you thought highly of them and another team drops them, now you can know what they may be worth). The cheat sheets come in especially handy at the end of the season for evaluating how well you did your rankings. Use them to determine which positions you are good at ranking and which need work. Do not feel too bad about your rankings being inaccurate. Generally 50% of the top 10 at most positions do not return each year due to injuries to themselves, teammates or their team issues (except Defenses, See Tip# 36).

53 League Trends

Determine in advance what has the highest probability of occurring in your league's draft. Research previous drafts using the same format (rules, starting rosters, etc), to get a feel for what to expect. For example, if drafting in the World Championship of Fantasy Football (WCOFF) for the first time, look at last year's drafts and determine the average position allocation. How many players from each position were drafted? This gives you an idea of how deep your rankings need to be. Analyze the trends from past drafts and pay particular attention to the winners' lineups, both coming out of the draft and their final roster. Sometimes the position allocation for one is different than the other. For example, most winning teams may draft 2 QBs, 7 RBs, 8 WRs, 1

TE, 1 K and 1 Defense on a 20 player roster. But they may finish with 2 QB, 6 RBs, 7 WRs, 2 TEs, 2 Kickers and a defense in order to cover the TE and Kicker in case of an injury or terrible match-up.

Other trends may be the order some positions are drafted. In the National Fantasy Football Championship (NFFC) for example, QBs are drafted higher than in the WCOFF because the NFFC awards 6 points for passing TDs. QBs are more valuable and thus drafted sooner. In the FFPC, TEs are awarded 1.5 points per reception and thus TEs are drafted higher than in either the NFFC or WCOFF. All of these trends should be available by looking at past drafts and lineups of the winners. This information may be online or you may have to request it from the league commissioner. Another useful place for trend data is the message boards of the league, where the history of the league may be posted as well as research others have performed.

54 Ignore contract year bias

The typical myth goes something like this: Players in the final year of their contract will play better because they want to show the other 31 teams (and their own) just what they can do in order to get a more lucrative contract. Do not buy into this. Every year in the NFL is a tryout. If you cannot be productive, you will not start in this league. It is all about winning and winning sooner rather than later. Some players excel in the final year of their contract, but there are just as many who perform average or worse. Do not let the fact that you remember a big name in his contract year do well (Or ESPN repeats that statistic repeatedly) bias you. **Most do not do significantly better.**

Chapter 4 Draft Strategies

55 Draft for the flex player

Know how many players can be used as a flex. Refer to Table XX Supply and Demand in Appendix B. Determine which position you will end up using as a flex realistically and make sure you have good players to fill the flex. The more teams in the league and the more RBs or flex players used, the less likely you will be using a RB as the flex player. Plan on using a WR as a flex on many occasions as there are not that many WRs.

56 Stud RB (Modified)

This strategy says that RBs win championships so get as many as you can- early and often. Ok, maybe not so much anymore. Still, RBs are the most limited position on the field. Realistically there are only 32 RBs (one per team) and so having 2 starters and maybe a third is a good strategy. Sure, there are only 32 QBs as well, but they tend to perform about the same after the top 8 or so. So QB9-QB25 is not that much different and can be obtained later in the draft. But there is a big difference between RB9 and RB25. **Draft a RB in the first round unless you have the 8th or later pick and want to grab a top 4 WR.** In this case, you can get a top 15 RB with your 2nd round pick.

57 Draft a RB then WR or a WR then RB with your first two picks

You can draft two RBs with your first two picks and get two starting RBs, but in doing so you have neglected the WR position and forced your hand in having to draft WRs the next 2 rounds. By the same token, you could draft 2 WRs with your first two picks and then be forced to draft 2 RBs with your next two picks. **Instead, draft a RB then WR or a WR then RB with your first two picks.** This way you diversify and get a stud at each position and are not forced into drafting a certain position with your next picks. For example, you draft Randy Moss in the first round (1.09) then grab Andre Johnson in the 2nd round (2.04). Now in the third round Brandon Marshall has slipped all the way to you at 3.09. You think he is a steal here and never imagined he would be available. But if you draft him that will be your third WR with no RBs and they are thinning out rapidly. You may be forced to pass on the best player to get a RB. If you had gone WR-RB you have the option of grabbing either a RB or WR with your third pick.

58 Draft RBs and WRs in the first 6 rounds. Others by exception

I draft RBs and WRs in my first six rounds. I do not overload at one position or the other (Like RB-WR-WR-WR) but instead try to have 2 of each after the fourth and 3 of each after the sixth round. This balance allows me to grab any value that falls in my lap from either position. I may even draft either a RB or WR in the seventh round. Think about it - after six rounds I have 3 starting RBs and three starting WRs. That represents my starters at both positions and a flex starter.

WRs are more abundant than either the QB or the RB position (heck there are 64 WRs who start) but they have the added bonus of points per reception (PPR) too. So in PPR leagues they need to be drafted early and often as well.

59 Stud WR (Modified)

Originally this strategy was to grab a stud WR in the first round and it expanded to drafting a WR in both the first and second rounds. Some are tempted by this if they have the last draft spots. You can draft two stud WRs with the 1.11 and 2.02 draft picks but I do not recommend this strategy. Why not? Because WRs are tied to the guy throwing them the ball. By drafting two WRs with your first two high draft picks, you have gambled too much on players who do not determine their own destiny. WRs can be hurt themselves or their QB can be hurt as well. So I consider them double risks to perform below expectations. For the same reason I never draft a QB-WR combo (Tip # 74). I do not draft WRs with both of my first two picks. Instead I suggest a modified Stud WR strategy where WRs are taken in the second and third round. You already have a stud RB and a stud WR from Tip # 57, now it is time to exploit that with another WR in round three. Of course, if a steal RB appears, then by all means draft him, but if all else is equal look to the WR pool. Why? WRs in the 3rd -5th round are the WR8-WR25 so you still get a good starter but do not pay too much for them. In a PPR league, these middle WRs will pay dividends.

60 Avoid being the last owner to get a starting QB

If you wait too long you may end up with your 14th or 15th ranked QB and then the drop off really starts as far as fantasy points are concerned. If you do delay and wait on your QB1, then you need to follow it up with your QB2 fairly quickly thereafter. In essence, if you passed on the quality QB early on, now you need to make up for it with additional starting QBs. Who do you target? See Tip # 86

61 DBC (Defense by Committee)

The old adage is do not draft a kicker or defense until the end of the draft. Generally this is true but some leagues give defenses more scoring by awarding points based on what their opponents score or how many yards they gain. In these types of scenarios defenses deserve more weight. But rather than reach for a defense in the first half of the draft (8-10th round) and sacrifice that important handcuff RB (Tip # 63) or fourth WR for use on bye weeks, try waiting and drafting two mediocre but complementary defenses. With this "rotating defense" approach, two average defenses are picked because they have easy matchups on alternating weeks, and thus, can provide the same points as a great defense.

Look for defenses outside the top 15 so that you can draft them without fear of another team grabbing your other half of the Defense By Committee. They should come from winning teams, as these are the defenses most likely to be leading during the game and able to force their opponents into definite passing situations. Look for teams that play several teams with bad defenses but on opposite weeks of each other. Finally, look for defenses that have a good chance to improve from last year's performance. Then you play the defense that has the best match up (plays the worst offense). In theory, by using the rotating defenses, you can achieve the same results as a top 10 defense.

62 Stockpile

Napoleon Bonaparte is famous for his quote "Quantity has a quality all its own." In essence, whatever position is weak among the big three (QB, RB and WR), now you need to make up for it with a large quantity of sleepers (Sleepers are players that are long shots but you are more optimistic than most owners about them). If, in the draft, you get some great players in one position and find yourself weak in the other. Shift the focus of your draft away from the strong position and draft more sleepers from the weak position, hoping to hit on one or two players who can become starters and shore up the weak position. Typically this occurs at either RB or WR, but if you wait too long to get a QB and he is not in the top 15, perhaps drafting three QBs will provide you with one that is a Top 10 QB. The same is true for RBs or WRs. If, due to the way the draft unfolds, you end up with 1 good RB and 3 good WRs and a strong QB, then the rest of the draft you should concentrate on adding depth at RB, so that hopefully one of them will develop into your RB2.

Stockpiling at RB or WR usually provides the best chance of hitting a sleeper. You are not cornering the market on RBs or WRs since there are realistically about 80 of each available. Instead, you are increasing your chance of finding that diamond in the rough of RB or WR if you have eight RBs or WRs.

63 Handcuff

Handcuffing is the process of drafting the backup for your stud players. You are handcuffing yourself to that player and his backup, hence the name. Normally this is done for RBs (your RB1 and maybe RB2) but on occasion it can be very beneficial to do for QBs. Think of handcuffing as buying insurance. You pay a premium price in that you cannot draft another player who may do better, but if your player goes down, for whatever reason, your insurance pays off in that the handcuff now becomes your starter.

Do not handcuff simply to handcuff. Make sure the backup is really the backup (i.e. he will take the place of the replaced player). Also just because he takes the field as the replacement does not necessarily mean he is worthy either. He needs to be capable of scoring fantasy points if he does get the chance. Another consideration is the vulnerability of the original player. If you draft a player who is "fragile" and has a history of injuries, you better handcuff him. Sometimes the price for a handcuff is expensive. Such is the case with Chester Taylor, Adrian Peterson's handcuff, because his capability is well documented and AP's health is questionable.

Handcuffing a QB can be dangerous in that you have to draft another QB to replace your two same team QBs on their bye week, so you are forced to draft three QBs. You may find that the cost of this insurance is too expensive. The backup is dead weight taking up a valuable roster spot on your team. This means one less sleeper makes it on to your roster and is therefore available for other owners. Look for QB handcuffs that have good potential if they find themselves in the job. If you draft a QB and his backup is just as good or competing strongly for the job, then drafting his handcuff (backup) is a way of insuring that, if an injury or demotion occurs, you will not have lost your starter.

64 Draft for an easy early season

This really is the antithesis of the draft for the fantasy football playoffs theory. In that strategy you draft players exclusively that should have a good fantasy football playoff run. If the league's playoffs run from week 14 through week 16, then those players facing easy opponents those three weeks would be given a premium. I DO NOT use this strategy. Matchups that look good in August have a tendency to look bad in December. Not only that, but players drafted in August may not even be starting in December due to injuries, coaching changes, teams taking a new direction after a losing record, or player trades.

If there should be any bias, it is for the first half of the season. Weeks 1-4 are when you start your studs and almost put the team on autopilot. No way do you take any chances and start a potential sleeper. Basically it takes a few weeks to shake out the season and see which teams are good and which are bad for whatever reasons. Week 4 is when you can start to massage your team to maximize matchups and trends. Week 4 is also when the bye weeks start. A fast start (4-2 or 5-1) based on drafting for an easy early part of the season puts you closer to the playoffs than starting slow (2-4 or 1-5) and hoping to make the playoffs so that your players can shine in those games.

Another reason I plan for the fast start is the drop off from some owners at the end of the season. I call this the "Dead Money syndrome". Some owners when they see they are out of contention for the playoffs (4-6 or worse with three games remaining) stop actively managing their rosters. Sometimes they still manage their rosters but just barely in that they replace the injured or the bye week players but do not get any free agents. In other cases, they are so busy with their other successful teams that they ignore the dead weight (Dead Money) teams. So who knows, maybe your schedule will allow you to play some dead money teams later in the season and that fast start in fact gives some added advantages.

You still need to perform well in the playoffs. But why draft a player based on how you think they will do four months or more from the draft? Better to plan on drafting players who should start and play well right away.

65 Draft Spot

You should know your draft spot well before draft day. If your draft assigns your draft spot at the last second - avoid this draft. You can plan and strategize and mock based on your draft position and this is one way to get some advantage. Your draft spot should determine your initial strategy for the first three rounds. If you have an early draft spot, RB is probably your first choice. In fact, RB is probably your first round choice for most of your draft spots with the exception of the last few and then grabbing a stud WR may be better if the RBs are not that strong.

No matter what, have a plan of attack. Know that you are going to draft RB-WR-RB based on mock drafts and the players who should be available to you at your draft spots.

66 Auction values as other tools

Even if you do not play in an auction league, you can still use the concept of auctions to assist in planning and playing fantasy football. Auction values are based on imaginary monetary amounts. But if the auction league has the same scoring rules and starters, then the auction values will be a great representation of where each player is ranked. Auction values are the perfect tool to use in tiering. If you are in doubt about five players and where they should go tier-wise, look at their auction values. Use the values to rank within tiers and to determine which tier a player should go into.

If you have to evaluate a trade, look at their auction values from before the draft. Sure, their values may have gone up or down since then, but it can give you a baseline to start evaluating. Acquiring players through free agency can also use auction values. But instead of using the $1 value for the player coming off waivers, think about where he would rank based on his projected value. If he is a RB who will now start due to an injury and you think he is likely to be a RB25 equivalent, then look at what the 25th RB had for an auction value. If he was worth $30 of a $200 budget, then he would be worth $150 in a $1000 FAAB (about the same percentage of your budget). But remember that was when you had to draft other players. So now, depending on which week of free agency you are in (week 1 versus the last week), the amount of your budget should be prorated. In other words, the amount you pay for a player will depend on how many more chances you have to aquire someone of that value. This is influenced by how many weeks of FA are left.

Finally, use auction values in general (overall player rankings) to evaluate draft spots as far as trades are concerned. If someone wants to trade you for the 10th and 20th overall picks, add up their auction values and compare them to the relative auction values of the spots you are offered.

Chapter 5 Draft Day Tips

67 RB early

Draft RBs early and often. Why? Because there are a limited amount of starting RBs and they perform to varying degrees. So having 2 of the "no kidding" starting RBs gives you a huge advantage over teams who can only draft 1 of the starters. But avoid the dreaded running back by committee (RBBC) situations, if possible. Even if you can get both RBs, try and avoid this situation. Even if you do have both RBs, you will have headaches trying to scour your resources for who will be the official starter, and even then just because they "start" does not mean they will be carrying the ball the most or scoring the most.

68 Avoid older RBs, especially those over 30

Avoid older RBs, ones over 30, as they are more likely to lose a step, have an injury or retire unexpectedly on you. Studies have shown that RBs peak from 23-25, they have slight declines from age 26-28 and after 28 they have pronounced declines. There are always exceptions but generally RBs start their decline at age 30 (28.5-31.5). Martin Signore mentions this in *Fantasy Football for Dummies*. "NFL rushing statistics show that RB production declines sharply after the age of 30. All the years of running, blocking, and taking hits really adds up, just like mileage on a car". On average they will miss 2 games a year, play for 12 years (only 10 are really good productive years) and carry the ball 275 times a year.

So be careful with RBs over 28 and avoid those over 30. Keep in mind that this is based on a normal workload. If the RB has had a reduced workload (i.e. back up RB with fewer carries for a year or two) then these ages can be extended appropriately. Speaking of carries……

69 Avoid RBs with 375 carries from previous season

Watch RBs with over 370 carries from the previous year. They tend to break down more often the next season. "Break downs" can be from major injuries or minor "nagging" injuries that do not keep him off the field but hamper his production (and lower his carries). RBs that catch lots of passes out of the backfield need to have their passes calculated as carries too. So **use one half of the catches as carries**. For example, if Matt Forte rushes 340 times in a season and catches 80 passes that would give him a total adjusted carry amount of 380 (340 + 80/2=340+40). Watch out for these players. Include the post season as well; if a team advances deep into the playoffs that can take a toll on a RB the following season. Generally, it will be easier for a younger RB to adapt (except for rookie RBs, more on them in a moment). The older the RB, the more carries and the more frequently they exceed 370 touches, all represent greater danger. Rookie RBs are not used to the NFL pace (more games than in college) and thus can tend to break down late in the season if they are carrying the ball more than they are used to. The following season may see some let down if they carried over 370 in their rookie season, because again, they are not used to the stamina required of an NFL season. Most rookies do not get that many carries their rookie season.

70 K Late

Grab a kicker with your next to last or last pick of the draft. A kicker's performance is too hard to predict from season to season. So much depends on who their team plays, how their defense performs, how the offense moves the ball, the head coach's philosophy, etc. The kicker is the one player who does not get on the field on their own. They only make the playing surface if someone else scores a TD or if the offense stalls in the opponents' territory. Unlike QBs, RBs, WRs and TEs who take the field on several possessions during the game, kickers may never have a chance to kick.

The difference between the #1 and #12 kicker is small. In many cases the difference between kicker #5 and #17 is less than a point per game. The top three kickers do perform significantly better than the other kickers, but determining who will be the top 3 kickers is problematic at best.

Avoid kickers until you just cannot stand it anymore - simple yet effective advice. Other tips have explained why they are hard to predict ranking wise (Tip #35). This tip simply tells you to avoid them until you absolutely have to draft them. So draft your one and only kicker in the last round. Who cares if you get the 15th kicker or the 22nd kicker? There is not that much difference in performance and you have just as much chance of getting a top 5 kicker. Do not waste too much time or energy on this low impact position.

Another great reason for picking kickers late is to avoid "possessiveness". If you reach for a kicker early you tend to feel like you have to hold him to prove that it was smart to take him so early. This psychological feeling is known as "endowment." If instead you pick up a kicker with your last pick, you are much more likely psychologically to be able to release him if he is not performing well. Owner A takes Shayne Graham with his last pick in the 20th round; Owner B takes Jason Elam in the 10th round. Both are ranked in the middle of the kickers mid-way through the season when a new kicker takes over due to injury at a top scoring team. Which owner will have an easier time releasing his kicker to add the new better kicker? The team with "less invested" in their current kicker.

Kickers on the waiver wire can be just as good as any found in the draft. Often a kicker that starts off well in the first few weeks of the season will continue the trend and have a good season. If they are available, dropping your late round kicker for the waiver wire prospect is not unrealistic.

71 QB Wait

QBs are dependable and score many points. Last year, the top seven QBs finished in the top 8 in terms of fantasy points scored. So you should draft a QB first, right? NO! What this means is that QBs score the most but they all score a ton of points so there is no reason to grab one of the top QBs. Just 30 points separated QB2 Jay Cutler from QB7 Matt Cassel (who, without a doubt, was not even drafted, but instead snatched off the waiver wire immediately after Brady went down) in 2008. 47 points separate QB8 and QB16; so about 90 points or 5 points per game separates the 2nd best QB and the 16th best QB. Those same 90 points are the difference between the same rankings at RB and WR. However, you start and thus need 3 RBs and 3 WRs. You only start 1 QB. The demand (or lack thereof) means QBs are available long after the RB and WR availability has dried up

Wait to draft your QB until the 5th round or later. If you do draft a QB earlier, you sacrifice a quality player at RB or WR. Only draft a QB earlier than the 5th if you are in a QB heavy league (start 2 QBs, or QBs can be a flex player or where QBs get 6 points for passing TDs) or if a top 4 QB falls in your lap in rounds 3 or 4. The difference between the #5 QB and #11 QB is 1 point per game on average in most 4 point per passing TD leagues. Why draft the 5th QB in the third round when you can solidify either the RB or WR position where studs are rapidly becoming in short supply? The #5 QB in the third round will not be significantly different than the #11 QB who can be drafted in the 6th or 7th round or maybe even later. Wait on drafting a QB until two thirds of the owners have a QB. In a 12 team league that means look for your QB after 8 QBs have been drafted (14 team leagues wait til 9 QBs are drafted). Now you must actively seek out your QB. Do not delay because some owners will get panicky and grab their second QB in these middle rounds.

Things change if in a league where QBs are awarded six points for a TD pass. Then QBs move up a bit, but still not much more, simply because the demand for them is less and the fact that they score more for a TD pass only puts a slightly higher premium on those QBs who throw more TDs (P. Manning, Drew Brees, etc).

The QB pool is deep and has lots of value later since you only start 1 QB and there are 32 of them versus RBs where you start at least 2 of them (maybe more in a flex league) and there are only 32 of them (more or less). The top QBs go in rounds 1-4 but rarely will an owner draft two QBs in the first eight rounds because this weakens his team at the other positions too much. Use this to your advantage. If the top seven or eight QBs are drafted early, why not wait and get one of the top ten after the rush on QBs ends. The difference between QB#6 and QB#10 is not going to be that much different but you can get one in the 4th round and the other in the 7th or 8th round. Which is better?

Another reason to wait on QBs is the turnover at the position recently, due to injuries. Tom Brady, Carson Palmer, Matt Hasselbach, and Mark Bulger all spring to mind when injuries are mentioned. Even the great Peyton Manning suffered a few slack games in 2008 while recovering from off-season surgery.

QBs rarely (if ever) repeat record-breaking seasons. So if Matt Ryan throws for 50 TDs, do not bank on him doing it again the next season. For this reason, many of the top QBs who are drafted in those early rounds are not worth the high price paid in terms of sacrifices at the other positions.

72 Ignore preseason primarily

There will be diehards that scoff at this tip, but for the most part you need to ignore the preseason and the hype that comes with it. There will be coaches touting certain star players, players making bold predictions (remember John Kitna predicting the Lions would win 10 games in 2007) about teams going undefeated but none of this has any bearing on what fantasy points those players produce. Just because Dominik Hixon has four TDs in one preseason game does not mean he will replace Plaxico Buress for the NYG in 2008. Take it all with a grain of salt. Yes, Dominik is someone to remember as a sleeper should Plaxico become injured or stray from the straight and narrow with the criminal justice system (both hard to believe I am sure), but he is not someone who is worthy of your WR3 spot. Be realistic in your preseason rankings. Just because the stud WR is only used for two series in two games does not mean that he is on the way out. Even his stats from those few starts may not reflect star status. Why the poor stats? Probably because he ducked out of bounds in those preseason games or did not run at top blazing speed. He does these things because he knows it is preseason and why risk an injury in preseason when it COUNTS FOR NOTHING!

Therefore, what should you use the preseason for, in terms of fantasy football? Watch the known position battles. If there are two QBs or RBs or Kickers competing, watch to see who looks better, who has the inside track and who bonds best with the coaches, starting QB or teammates. Look at the third preseason game as an indicator of who is the starter. Usually the last preseason game is for the backups and players trying to make the team. Game 3 of the preseason is for the starters to play a half and get into season shape.

Another important aspect of the preseason is to monitor injuries. Injuries can move some players up your ranking (if the player ahead of them on the team depth chart is injured) or down depending on the injury. The preseason is also a great opportunity to monitor existing injuries or the recovery of them. LT and Antonio Gates in the 2008 preseason did not look like their usual selves, this was a big hint to lower each in the rankings.

Finally, the biggest benefit of the preseason is finding sleepers. You may have already identified them, but now you can see how they progress. Many times the player who will replace a stud in the lineup gets his playing time or try out in the preseason. D. Hixon was one such example. If you remembered him from the preseason, or drafted him late as a sleeper on the off chance that Plaxico misbehaved, you were rewarded in the games where he started. By following the preseason you were alerted to his potential.

The bottom line is to not get too excited about the stats, starts or records coming from the preseason. It is make believe and does not count for anything. Coaches and teams use the preseason to evaluate player potential, injuries and rookies. You should do the same.

73 Use a draft tracker

Too many times, I see owners keep track of nothing but their own team. They just write down which players they have drafted but have no idea who needs which positions. By keeping track of what others have done, you can predict what they will do in future rounds. You do not have to keep track of the actual names of players drafted by your opponents. Instead, **track which positions and how many they have drafted**. For example, if only one other team needs their first QB along with you and you have three QBs left in your tier, then you can skip a QB in the current round and focus on other position needs. You can still pick up your first QB from that tier in a later round. It does not matter which of those three QBs in the tier you draft, just that you get one of them because they are all the same (TIP #45 Tiers). On occasion I see owners go overboard and track all the players drafted by other teams. I do not recommend it. Do not do this as it just wastes valuable draft time. Sure, you can cross the player's name off your cheat sheet, but rely on the draft board for those exact name details and instead use a simple draft tracker to track trends.

See Appendix A Draft Tracker

74 Avoid QB/WR Combos

If there are three WRs to choose from, all in the same tier, do not draft one from the same team as your QB1. Avoid if possible players with the same bye week as RB1or RB2. All of this is because I want consistent points. The points lost are negated somewhat by the backup. Say I lose 15 points and my backup is good for 10 points. In effect, I see a decrease of 5 points at that slot when my WR is on his bye. If I combine that loss with another letdown at QB (because both have the same bye week) then my loss may be another 3 points. Now I am down 8 points because of the combination. If I combine that 8-point loss with RB1 or RB2 on the same bye week, that is about a 15-20 point reduction. Losing 20 points is a guaranteed loss that cannot be made up. If I spread those point reductions over six games (QB1, RB1, RB2, WR1, WR2, W3) then my team is only losing a few points every week and I have a better chance of overcoming each reduction.

Another reason for avoiding the combo is if the QB gets hurt then the WR will probably lose some productivity. Think back to what happened to Steve Smith when J. Delhomme went down with an injury for a few weeks in 2006 and Randy Moss in 2008 when Tom Brady was lost to injury. Don't use any combos and do not get starters on the same bye week. It also goes without saying that you should not draft more than two players from the same team (not counting kickers). This can mean that if the QB or RB is hurt, the others may suffer too.

75 Draft conservatively early and aggressively late

You cannot win your league in the draft, but you can lose it. If you take too many chances in the early rounds, you can really torpedo any chance of a winning team. Sure, you may come away with a great team 1 out of 10 times, but those are long odds in my book. When I say conservatively I mean – draft first half conservative, draft last half aggressively with deep sleepers - take chances that might payoff since they are the scrubs anyway.

76 Players to devalue (avoid)

Never avoid any player completely unless he is injured and out for the season. However, there are players that need to be devalued based on "issues" they have. Players who have a new system should be devalued. It can be that the player is traded to a new team, has a new head coach or has to learn a new system. All mean a learning curve is more than likely the first year out. These same players are usually overvalued on draft day because of perceived new synergies from the change; when, in fact, it takes some time to develop chemistry among the players asked to do new things. Trouble-makers also need to be devalued. The league does not put up with the "bad boy" mentality any longer. These players are more likely to be suspended in the future and for longer periods of time than a first offender. Devalue them appropriately.

77 Draft discriminators

If you find yourself trying to decide between two equal players on draft day, use the following discriminators to make the decision. Avoid players who are injury prone. If your choice is between two RBs, go with the one who has been injured the least. Avoid players with byes on the "big" bye weeks (weeks where more teams are on byes). Pick the player from the offense that is more explosive. Avoid players on the same team (diversification). Finally, look for players with favorable fantasy playoff schedules. If your league has the playoffs in week 15 and 16, use players who play weak teams in those weeks as a discriminator. You will find that when you make the playoffs you win more often.

78 Have a plan

My dad always said, "Do something, even if it turns out to be wrong." I agree with him now that I am a little older (OK, a lot older). Sometimes doing the wrong thing is better than doing nothing at all. If you start out with the wrong plan you can change the plan later (flexibility) and still reach the same objective.

However, if you never start the process or worse, start the process with no idea where you want to be at the end, you could end up never reaching your goal. If you have a goal it is easier to know if you are approaching it, or else you end up flailing around hopelessly lost. What we mean is have a plan. The worst thing you can do is walk into the draft without a game plan. Use a draft theory or system. It does not really matter which one you use as long as it is based on sound advice. The point is you need a road map to follow initially. It could all go pear shaped by round five, but if it does you should still know how far along you are toward your goal and the plan will give you some idea of how to go about getting there after your detour. For example, your plan is to draft a QB late (Tip #71). You draft RB-WR-WR-RB and then in the 5th round, for some reason, Tony Romo is still available (the drafter ahead of you is a Redskins fan and has vowed never to draft a Cowboy -lucky you). So with the first pick of the 5th round (5.01) you draft Tony Romo. This is a great steal for you but it changes your plan. Now instead of targeting a QB mid rounds (and maybe two at that) you have that square filled and have to concentrate on adding better WRs to make up for your lack of strength there (since you go RB with pick 6).

Without a plan, you could have gone RB-WR-WR-WR-QB and now are faced with no RB2. Sure a strong WR position but lots of weakness at RB if your RB2 is drafted in the 6th round.

79 Bye weeks

There are two schools of thought here and I have played them both. One is that you should plan for bye weeks and make sure you have contingency plans for them. These contingency plans involve avoiding drafting starters with the same bye week, if possible, and making sure you have backups who have good matchups when they do start for you (due to the starter on a bye week). The other strategy is to try and get all of your players on the same bye week. If all of your starters are essentially on a bye in only one week, you will be much stronger in the 6 other weeks.

You sacrifice one week (the week most of your team is on a bye) but you are a stronger team the other 6 weeks and that should give you a little edge.

Let's start with the first strategy "Bye week avoidance." Start by planning for them. If you know you have an early draft pick, use that knowledge and the players available and their bye weeks to your advantage (the 4th pick in the draft and the first three picks are "no brainers"), to make the choice between one player or another. If you really want a certain QB or RB and his bye week is the same as one of the players you can choose from in the first round, then "plan" on not taking that early RB and go with your other choice. You have just prevented a bye week conflict before the draft.

Always list the players' bye weeks on your cheat sheets (See Appendix C Cheat Sheets Sample-QB). You must have the bye week knowledge at your finger tips because sometimes you narrow down which position to draft with most of your allotted draft time and the remaining time is devoted to deciding between two players at the same position. No use wasting valuable time trying to look up in a magazine or ask your fellow owners what bye week. As a fail safe back up measure always list the bye weeks and the teams on them on a copy of the NFL schedule that you bring to the draft. Fantasy Football Almanac: The Essential Fantasy Football Reference Guide (www.FFGuidebook.com/almanac) always lists the NFL schedules and then the NFL Bye Week List. Make sure you have your copy for the draft or a simple one page NFL schedule and write down the bye weeks at the top with the teams on each week.

Track the other teams' bye weeks too using a draft tracker (Tip #73 draft tracker; see also Appendix A Draft Tracker). If you know that one owner is drafting most of his starters from the same bye week, it will help you "predict" who they will draft each round. In the 4th round if they have drafted RB-WR-WR and all were week 8 bye teams, then I would expect him to draft a RB on bye week 8. You can use that prediction to help make your decision.

Remember the bye weeks are not evenly distributed either. In 2008 weeks 4 and 8 had six teams on a bye. The remaining five weeks (5-7, 9-10) had only four teams on byes. If you are going to avoid bye conflicts - lots of starters on the same bye - why not also avoid the bye weeks where more players are out? In other words, use as a discriminator and avoid if possible, those players on the bye weeks with more teams. In 2008 that would mean targeting players on bye weeks other than week 4 and 8 and avoiding players from those team heavy bye weeks.

If you want an easier strategy, which works just as well, try drafting players from the same bye week. In other words, you load up on starters who share the same bye week so that you can minimize the bye week effect for the rest of the season. It may start with your draft plan. If you have an early pick and can pretty much draft whomever you want with your first pick, then you can look down the road and see who you would like to target at QB, RB, WR and TE. If players you like all have the same bye week, then perhaps your plan will be to target each of those players individually. Realize that by doing this you may have to abandon a true VBD (see Tip # 96), but the reward can be a stronger team, if successful. Obviously, you will not be able to draft all of your preferred players from the same bye week. You may only get a QB, RB and TE but that may be enough of an advantage to boost your performance by a few points in those critical bye week games. Remember that which ever week the majority of your starters are out (the bye week that most of your players are on) your team will be weaker than most. Expect a loss on that 'throw away" week. But also give it your best shot by picking backups who have the best chance of a big game that one week, based on their schedule. Do not worry about Kickers or Defenses and their bye weeks. These positions are so indifferent in their performances that drafting them simply on bye week is a waste of time.

I have used both the "avoid bye weeks" and "plan to all be on the same bye week" strategies. I prefer the avoid bye weeks strategy, but sometimes your hand is played for you. I played in the inaugural Fantasy Football Players Championship (FFPC, www.theFFPC.com) in 2008 (League 13, Neptune) and found myself with Reggie Wayne in the 2nd round and Peyton Manning fell in my lap with the 11th pick of the 4th round (4.11). So I drafted Peyton and with my 5th round pick (5.02) found Dallas Clark. I added Marvin Harrison in the 6th round (6.11) to shore up the WR position. After six rounds I have RB-WR-RB-QB-TE-WR and four of the six are on bye week 4. I did not plan on this, it just happened when Peyton Manning fell into my lap in the 4th. By picking Peyton, I violated Tip #74, never draft a QB-WR combo. Now I have 2 of my 4 studs on the same bye week. With Dallas Clark available, I decided to change the plan and go with a "as many players on same bye week" plan. I finished with the 2nd highest points in League 13 and finished 7th overall in the Main Event Championship.

Having said all of that, I still prefer the "avoid bye week conflicts." If you go "all in" and try to get the same bye week for the majority of your starters, you will inevitably have members of the same team (see my example above),which breaks my general rule of diversification (Tip #161).

80 Draft prep

I cannot emphasize this one enough. Prepare for the draft like you were going into battle (which you are). The NFL coaching/scouting staffs do not call their NFL draft rooms the "war room" for nothing. You are trying to out smart every other owner at the draft. The best way to do that is to be more prepared than they are.

You should know every player who will be drafted. If a name is announced that you do not know, it better come from some homer who is picking his favorite WR who will never come off the practice squad all year.

If you mock draft enough you should see every player that will be drafted. When you do the mock drafts and a player is drafted that you do not recognize, do some homework on him. Research him. Why was he drafted and how high? This gets you in on the ground floor of potential sleepers. Most of these unknowns will not pan out. But a few are your ticket to success.

In 2006 while in Las Vegas for the World Championship of Fantasy Football (WCOFF, www.WCOFF.com), I watched a big entry draft after the Thursday kickoff game. In that draft someone took Marques Colston WR. I went back to my hotel room and did some research on the stranger. Turns out he was 7th round draft pick from Hofstra, but he was moving up the rankings pretty fast. I did not get a chance to grab him in my auction league the following day, but as I reviewed the other draft boards (Tip #185) I saw his name several times. To make a long story short (too late) I missed out on getting him by one draft spot (the owner next to me took him right before me) and he went on to have a great rookie season (8 TDs and over 1000 yards). **So do mock drafts and listen for those players you do not know or have not ranked and then research them.**

Another good way to prepare for the draft is to map out a mock draft in your league based on past tendencies. Every year do the WRs usually fly off the board in round 4? Do QBs go in round 6? If so, do a mock draft on paper to see where players might go this year. It will give you a better understanding of what may happen. Use the past three drafts and how many positions are drafted in each round to determine how many players go and where.

81 Know and exploit the rules

The number one mistake in fantasy football is not knowing the rules. When we talk rules we mean drafting method, time limits, penalties for missing pick, scoring rules and starters/roster limits. At the 2006 World Championship of Fantasy Football, one of the owners leaned over and ask me how many WRs we started in the league. If you do not know that by the time you sit at the draft, you are in big trouble. But to give them some credit, better to find out right before the draft or even a few rounds into the draft than after the draft. As it was, he found out in round 8 after loading up on everything but WRs. He had some catching up to do at WR.

Knowing the rules is one thing, using that to your advantage is another. In 2008, in one of the Expert drafts I participated in (www.Expertsdraft.com), I noted that the rules stated I had to start a kicker and defense but not that I had to draft a kicker or a defense. Therefore, while everyone else drafted a kicker or two and a defense or two with their late picks I drafted extra RBs and WRs. After it was all over, a few of the other owners made some comments about me not drafting any Ks and Defenses. I explained that I would drop two of my sleeper players that had not panned out, right before the first week deadline and add a kicker and defense from the free agency list since only 13 or so of each were drafted. My rationale was a kicker or defense in the last two rounds would not be that much different than one picked up in free agency and I would rather draft some long shots and see how they played out since our draft was very early in the preseason (June, I think). This story does not have a happy ending as I had the 12th draft pick and my team was decimated by injuries to Tony Romo, Kevin Curtis, Joey Galloway and Willie Parker. Oh and Edge let me down too. But I digress. Moving on…

Some other examples of knowing the rules include: If your league does not require a TE as a starter (only as a flex player), you will kick yourself after drafting two lesser TEs in the middle rounds. If your league starts two WRs, you can concentrate less on WRs than if the league starts 3 WRs. Finally, if your league allows changes in the roster right up until game time, you can make roster moves affected by the latest NFL news on game day. If you hear from John Clayton that Reggie Bush is out for the game today, then go change your roster and put in someone else.

Anyone will be better than Bush who is sitting on the pine this afternoon.

What if you have wrapped up the #1 seed and you can influence the #4 seed that you will play next week in the playoffs? For example, you are playing a team that if they win they will be the #4 seed and play you again next week. Do you "tweak" your roster to allow them a better chance of winning? Perhaps some injured players make it onto your roster that week instead of a stud. Some say this is morally wrong; you should always field the best team. Others insist it is within the rules and you are only doing what you can within the rules to win. I tend to be in the latter camp. As long as you put a player at each position I am fine with that exploitation of the rules.

Do you have a flex position? If so will more RBs be picked in the early rounds than normal? Many owners will draft according to starter positions. They will pick their starting QB, two starting RBs, two starting WRs and starting TE in the first six rounds. In other words, by getting a QB and TE earlier than you, they leave lots of good RBs and WRs for you to draft as flex players/backups/bye week replacements/trade bait. Then you can grab a serviceable QB and TE in rounds 7 and 8. Many owners like the QB position, although it isn't the most important in most leagues. Therefore, inexperienced owners will draft a QB early (rounds 2-4) and may get a QB2 in round 7, so watch for a run/depletion on QBs in these leagues.

Why do I need to know my scoring system? Whether QBs are awarded 3 or 6 points per passing TD, will determine how valuable P. Manning is. If your league awards points for yardage and/or points per reception, then some players are more valuable than others who catch TDs but do not get the large yardage or catches.

82 Do not get caught up in position runs

Every draft is different but every draft has position runs. What is a run? When, in any given round or succession of picks, a certain position is picked predominantly. For example, if in the 5th round you have the last pick (12th) and 6 of the last 9 picks have been QBs, then that would qualify as a QB run. It will naturally make you want to grab a good QB before they are all gone. Runs are powerful psychological forces. You say to yourself, "Everyone else
is getting a QB, I do not want to miss out. They must know what they are doing."

AVOID THIS MENTALITY! You have a plan (Tip # 78). You know when to draft a QB or whatever position is running. Suggest or start a run by saying aloud "Hmmm… looks like a lot of QBs are being picked," or the less obvious, "Here comes the TE run." Let the lemmings of the group chase after these runs and be reactive. You are going to be proactive and get value with every pick. Runs occur when owners begin to pick the same position with pick after pick after pick. This develops into a herd mentality. I have to get my TE before everyone else gets his or her TE. Do not fall into this trap. It will make you abandon your strategy and lose value in the draft. If you know what position and players you are going to target in round six (WR3) it should not matter that four TEs in a row have been drafted ahead of you; it only helps you now, in that a better WR may be around.

Many times these position runs occur at about the same time from year to year and league to league (especially if they use the same rules). In a 12-team, PPR league with points for yardage too, RBs go in the 1st and 2nd rounds. WRs tend to go in the 3rd and 4th (with some TEs too). Then QBs see some mini runs in the 5th, 7th and 8th rounds. Kickers and Defenses have their runs much later in the draft.

83 Forget the past....sometimes

Don't get stuck in the past. Some owners love veterans even to the point of drafting them when they are past their prime. You need to evaluate all of the talent: old and new. Don't get stuck and find yourself saying "Well Bubba Franks is always good for a few TDs." Know before you draft if they are worth it. Do not rely on name and past performance only.

84 Avoid rookie enthusiasm/hype

Avoid the rookies or do not draft them too high. "Big City" always reminds me of the draft where he took E. James as a rookie with his second pick. Occasionally rookies will pay off big, but my question back to him is "Was he worth a second round pick?" The answer is no. If he had gotten him in the fourth round that year then he would have been a steal, but traditionally rookies do not produce big. Rather, they are over-hyped and drafted too high. Avoid rookies and the mess (underperforming against high expectations) they bring to a fantasy team. Some "experts" say that you should never draft a rookie as high as 25th overall, while others recommend no higher than 35th. I disagree with both. Draft a rookie where his rankings project him, just realize that, at best, he will perform at that level, but not any higher.

85 Target Breakout players

Breakout players are different from sleepers. A sleeper is someone who is relatively unknown and who performs much better than his draft position. So what defines "performs much better?" A QB in the "middle of the pack" ranking-wise who finishes in the Top 5 is a sleeper. A WR drafted in the last half of the draft who finishes in the Top 10 is one as well. I say to be a sleeper he has to be drafted in the bottom half of the fantasy starters and finish in the top 40%. Sleepers generally are undervalued, unproven rookies, has-been players or those players recovering from injury who are not expected to return to form.

What is a breakout player? A player who rushes or receives for over 1000 yards and eight or more TDs is my breakout player. That would put them roughly as a Top 15 RB or WR in most leagues, with 100 points for the yardage (1 point per 10 yards) and 48 more points for the TDs. These players are not sleepers but rather solid, more middle of the road players, who you expect to "breakout" and have a much better season. Expect 4-6 new WRs in the Top 15 each year. Breakout QBs will have at least 20 TDs and 3200 yards and make the Top 12.

For all positions, look for the breakout players (2nd-4th years) who have either learned the system, came on strong in the second half of last year, acclimated to a new team or grasped the system or QB. These players will give you that little bit extra to make the playoffs and win the Super Bowl.

86 Breakout QBs

How do you find a breakout player? QBs are most likely to break out in their 3rd and 4th years of play. QBs who hold the clipboard for 1-2 years perform better in a starting role than those thrust onto the field prematurely; although Matt Ryan and Joe Flacco in 2008 are the exceptions to the rule. They started on teams that were well-established and had good running games (strong RBs and good offensive lines). Both factors help rookie-starting QBs.

87 Breakout RBs

RBs only need two things: talent and opportunity. Opportunity comes from having a good OL and getting the chance to start. One of the three top-drafted rookie RBs will break out. However, most will break out in their 2nd-4th year, depending on opportunity. The first RB drafted in the NFL draft is a stud 80% of the time (recent ones include Ronnie Brown, Reggie Bush, Adrian Peterson and Darren McFadden). The percentages drop dramatically after that. Look for second half wonders – RBs who had a good second half (increased their Fantasy Points Per Game (FPPG) by 40% or more) will do well in the next year if they stay healthy and are a starter. Look for high yards per carry the previous season (4.2+), as this attracts attention from the coaches.

88 Breakout WRs

Look for a WR that had lots of receptions and good yardage the year before (50+ receptions and 850 yards). This is true for any WR, regardless of his years in the league. Look for WRs in their 2nd-5th year (who are 1st round NFL picks) who had 40+ receptions, 2+ TDs, 400+ yards and that are the starters (WR1 or WR2) on their team. They should have a consistent QB throwing to them and be completely free of injury. **WRs have a 25% chance of breaking out in either their 2nd, 3rd or 4th year.** With a 75% chance of breaking out in one of those three years, the longer the career the greater the chance of having a breakout year. Some break out in the 5th year as well, but breakout seasons after that are rare.

Rookie WRs rarely (5% of the time) break out. Rookies who do well in their first year (50+ receptions and 700+ yards) tend to break out the next year. Many first year QBs will concentrate on one WR they can trust and go to him often during the season. This WR is usually on the same side as the passing hand of the QB; if he is right-handed, then the WR on his right side will more than likely be his go-to-guy. But **QBs learn to spread the ball around more as they get more experience**.

Another attribute for a breakout WR is breakaway speed. Every WR in the NFL should be able to catch the ball; if they couldn't, they wouldn't have been drafted. But few have the acceleration that qualifies as breakaway speed. Also look for a WR with confidence. Think Chad Johnson, T.O., S. Smith and M. Harrison. Finally, look for dedication to the craft. Look for the WRs who arrive early and stay late; the ones who practice in the off-season with their QB or take extra time before every game to practice with their QB. As with RBs – WRs who had a good second half (increased their FPPG by 40% or more) will do well in the next year if they stay healthy and are a starter.

Some authors suggest avoiding free agent WRs all together. Instead of this "throwing out the baby with the bathwater theory" why not look at the reasons for the move in more detail. There are four major reasons why a WR shows up at another team. One he is too old and has been released because he has lost a step (think Marvin Harrison in 2009). Another reason may be for cap reasons (T. Owens in 2009 from Dallas). Still another is a WR whose contract has expired and wants out (TJH in 2009 when he went to SEA). The final reason is a trade where he is simply moved by his old team. In many of these cases, the WR may not be a good pick, but in some cases he can be a great pick if in the right system. So **do not ignore a WR who has switched teams, but evaluate him closer than one who has stayed in the same system.**

89 Breakout TEs

TEs have fewer breakouts than WRs simply because they get fewer looks for the all-important TD and fewer chances to break a long one when they are coming over the middle. But if you were attempting to predict the next John Carlson or Owen Daniels, look for 2nd-4th year TEs on a team with no "go-to WR" or combo WRs (Good WR1 and WR2) (think John Carlson TE SEA in 2008). They will be on a team with a good offense, where he is a starter and has good hands. Characteristically they are 6' 4" or taller and 250 lbs.

90 Have the latest information before you start the draft

Before you head to the draft, you need to know who is starting, who is hurt and who is holding out. Who is starting seems obvious, but too many owners do not update their cheat sheets with this last minute information. If a team has named a QB or RB the starter, they need to move up the rankings while the loser in the position battle moves down the rankings. Likewise, the kicker who is named the starter gets a spot on my cheat sheets and the one he beat out goes to the bottom. Sometimes these position battles are not worked out until just before the regular season starts, so stay up-to-date.

Injuries are another "must know" category. If a player hurt himself in practice and is out four long weeks, that will lower his stats by 25%. He needs to move down your rankings appropriately and his replacement moves higher. If a QB has not recovered as fast from an offseason injury or goes down in the last preseason game; it will affect the WRs. Always ensure your rankings/cheat sheets reflect the most current starter/injury data. Check your news sources just before entering the draft room or leaving for the draft.

Holdouts you know well in advance (already annotated on your rankings) and thus are not as time critical as an injury or benching, but the ending of a holdout instantly changes the dynamics of that position. Update your rankings as soon as the holdout ends. **Holdouts are more unpredictable then recoveries from injuries, so stay away from these players unless they are a bargain.**

Holdouts do not practice with the team and will require some time to get it together with their teammates after they return. Rookie holdouts are the worst. They will be set back a lot. Veterans can practice on their own and recover quicker than a rookie recovers. Do you draft the holdout and hope he comes to his senses or do you pass on him and risk missing his production if he returns? Holdouts are worse than injuries because you never know when a holdout will return, if at all. With an injury, you can get an estimate and then add a game to be conservative. Holdouts (HOs) are unknowns. I stay away from them. Let someone else take the chance on them with an early pick. Gambling is better for the later rounds.

91 Do not DRINK AND DRAFT

The casinos in Las Vegas give out free booze for a reason. It impairs your ability to think straight. Thus, you should give out booze freely on draft day. Bring a case of beer for the others but do not drink any yourself until after the draft. Why would you spend all your time and energy trying to be the best owner and then drink yourself into a weak spot?

Alcohol impairs judgment and leads to poor decisions. Distractions at the draft can also lead to poor decisions. Use distractions to your advantage, but do not get distracted by others. If someone starts talking about how great a player is going to be this year, tune them out. He is just talking to be talking and distracts you from studying the draft trends so far in the draft.

Even if you are going to drink and do get distracted, you can at least be rested before you show at the draft. All this requires getting a good night's rest the night before. An all-nighter the night before the draft only adds to the drag on your nerves when draft time finally comes. Again, you have waited almost 8 months for the draft to come around again, why waste the moment and all your offseason hard work with an all-nighter the night before and copious amounts of alcohol at the draft. If you want to win, let the other guys drink and draft.

92 Do not draft your entire lineup first then get backups

Too many owners draft every starter first before getting their backups. If the league starts 1 QB, 2 RBs, 2 WRs, 1 TE, 1 K and 1 Defense, do not draft each of them with your first eight draft picks. Kickers and defenses are not as important as getting a backup RB or WR or QB for those bye weeks or to replace him when an injury occurs. Which would you rather have, a Top 30 RB to replace your hurt #1 draft pick or a Top 5 kicker for the season? **Draft the high point position starters (RB and WR) first, then target their backups and then look at a starter QB.**

The QBs just do not provide as much value as a good RB or
WR on a bye week or to fill in for an injured starter.

93 Keep alert for entire draft

This tip involves not letting your guard down after the
break at the middle of the draft. Do not get a cold, refreshing beer
and sit back on your laurels. The middle rounds are where you
start to set yourself apart from the other owners. The early draft is
predictable and conservative, to a point. You have your overall
cheat sheet and you draft using VBD (Tip #96). Many leagues will
take a breather (although I hate breaks) after round eight or half
way through a draft, after round ten. This is just about the time
that your overall list of 100-120 players is empty. Now it is time
for team needs over VBD.

Remember the rule that only approximately 50% of the
Top 12 at any position make it back the following year. Where do
the other players that make it to the top come from? The middle
rounds! After eight or more rounds, you should have 1 QB, 3+
RBs, 3+ WRs, and 1 TE. No kickers or defenses as they come in
the late rounds. All of your primary starters are filled and you
have a backup at each of the low supply positions (RB and WR).
Now is the time to think about landing your handcuff for RB1
(Tip # 63). Plan on when you should take him based on his ADP
and a little proactive maneuvering.

You will need a QB2. Draft the one that starts versus the
hopeful super star. You will need a QB backup that can score you
points on the primaries bye week (or heaven forbid longer, if an
injury strikes), not the zero point rookie holding the clipboard
waiting for his chance to shine. Draft back ups who are on the
way up versus on the way down. Aging veterans rarely
outperform, but younger (2nd-4th year) players, if given the
opportunity, can be great sleepers. Upside potential and
opportunity are the keys in the middle rounds. Avoid players on
new teams as it may take some time for them to adjust, instead

look to teams that lost a veteran, as the replacement who comes from the team roster (who played with the team last year) has a better chance of shining.

The late rounds are for a K, DEF, low-end TE, sleepers and rookies. There are no gifts in FF. You need to concentrate hard on the middle and last rounds of the draft too, because when the injury bug comes, nothing will save you except a solid core of backups. Sleepers, rookies and breakout players are for the second half of the draft.

Spend more of your time looking at the middle to lower ranked players than the top players (the top 10 at RB or WR, top 5 at QB or TE) at each position. Say what? You heard me right. Spend some time on the top players at each position but spend more time looking at the others who will be drafted in the middle to late rounds. This is what separates the men from the boys, the newbie from the expert, the winners from the losers. Anyone can draft a top 10 RB or WR. Heck, most of your customized draft boards or cheat sheets are going to be pretty much the same. Of those 10 RBs you have, the other 11 owners probably have 90% of them in their top 10, just ranked a little (very little) differently. So are you really going to get a steal in the first four rounds? No. Can you mess up? Sure, but only by drafting a stud who just got hurt. But you can get some great value in the middle rounds by digging deep into that player grouping.

94 Uncertainty is good, risk is bad

Uncertainty creates great value at the draft. If a player is hurt or holding out, owners tend to go to extremes with their projections. Owners often err by confusing uncertainty with risk. Just because a player is holding out and his future is uncertain does not mean drafting him is risky. Where you draft them determines the risk you take, not his uncertain future. Some of my best value plays have been players with highly uncertain futures but with little risk of derailing my draft because I added them late in the draft as a sleeper. If they failed to do anything, I have not lost anything because that is what a sleeper normally does. The fact that I did not waste a high draft pick on the player cushions me against permanent team damage due to his flop. So it really is a situation where I either win or do not lose much. Those are the kinds of situations where others stay away and you can profit.

One such example is Cedric Benson in 2008. The Chicago Bears dropped him and no other teams were interested in him. I drafted him late in most drafts as a sleeper. He came through as CIN picked him up and he started as their RB. Great value for little cost.

95 Think about Supply and Demand

Look at Appendix B, the Supply and Demand table. If you need to determine which position to draft, think about how many players are available at the start of the draft (supply). Supply numbers are fixed until the NFL increases the number of teams playing each year. Now calculate how many players will be drafted from that position (demand); the more teams in the league or the greater the number of starters at that position, the larger the demand. If there are not enough players to go around than that position is more valuable if you can draft from it. This simply explains why RBs and then WRs are drafted first in the draft and why Kickers and Defenses are drafted late.

96 Use Value Based Drafting (VBD) in your first 100 picks

In 1996, Value-Based Drafting, a system for estimating player worth, was introduced into the fantasy football world by Joe Bryant (VBD was originally designed for baseball). VBD determines the value of a player, not by how much he scores, but by how much he outscores the other players at his position. Once that is known, you can compare players at other positions to one another. No longer will you be stuck with the dilemma of who to pick: your #8 QB or #25 RB? VBD gives you the answer.

In VBD, a player gets "value" by being better than the player who would take his place if he were lost for the season. So if A. Gates (the #1 TE in a 12-team league) is out for the season, who would take his place (if available on the free agent listing)? The #13 TE since TE2 through TE12 are on other teams. A. Gates should not be valued based on his projected fantasy points total for the upcoming season, but instead should be valued on how many points he will outscore the player who would have to replace him if he got hurt for the year. By using VBD every year, you value every player based on his projected fantasy point total minus the fantasy point total of the player who would replace him (called a baseline player). VBD doesn't encourage you to take the highest scoring player left on your cheat sheets, but the player who is projected to outscore the others at his position by the most points.

To explain VBD, an example is in order. Let's say you are in a two-team league that only starts a QB and a RB and you know in advance how many points each player is going to score this year (you have a time machine and you use it to cheat). You pick first and have a choice between P. Manning (#1 QB) who will score 250 points in your league, T. Brady (#2 QB- 230 points), LT (#1 RB- 200 points) or Steven Jackson (RB#2- 160 points). Who do you pick?

Most people would say P. Manning because he scores more points than all the others do. Let us see how your draft goes. You pick P. Manning. I pick LT. I pick T. Brady and you grab S. Jackson with the last pick. How many points will your team score this season?

Team Thumpers	Team Slam
P Manning 250	LT 200
S Jackson 160	T Brady 230
Total Points 410	Total Points 430

Now which team would you rather own? The idea behind VBD is that you need to outscore your opponent by as many points as possible, so you try to draft players that will outscore the others at their positions. If you have more players outscoring your opponents by more points, you should win. If you only wanted the highest scoring players, then your team would be filled with QBs and kickers, who score the most in fantasy leagues. VBD uses your starting lineup requirements and scoring system to develop cheat sheets. It also helps to avoid players that you may have drafted too early based on their stats, but that are not worth it so early in the draft based on your scoring system and rules.

Some draft strategies do not take your starting lineup requirements into account other than to compensate for more RBs if starting more and the same with WRs. VBD does much more. Before VBD, it was next to impossible to compare players at different positions. You could look at your projections for points and pick the player who should score the most (most common thing to do) but that really did not compare a RB to a WR. You were, at best, comparing the scoring of all RBs to all WRs, but not individual worth. VBD provides a method for valuing (hence the name) and comparing individual players from different positions. VBD estimates the relative value, and thus draft position, of different players at different positions based on the scoring system and the starters involved. Combining VBD with tiering and your opponent's needs can be a powerful drafting tool.

How do you calculate VBD? Take the player's total expected fantasy points (TP) and subtract the fantasy points of the player who would replace him, called the baseline player. The remaining number is a player's X points. X points are the same between all players, so a QB with 10 X points is the same value as a TE with 10 X points. Rank the players overall based on their X value not the total fantasy points they are expected to score.

97 Use the 100 Pick Method for a baseline

Baselines, or the player used to calculate a position's X points, can vary from strategy to strategy. Some owners just use the worst starter. If your 12-team league starts 1 QB, then the 12th ranked QB is the baseline. Some owners use the first back up (also called the "Worst starter +1"). In the QB example above, the baseline would become QB 13 (QB 1-12 are the starters and QB13 would be the one to replace an injured QB). See *Fantasy Football Guidebook, Chapter 10 Advanced Draft Theories* for more on baselines.

Use the 100 Pick Method for determining each position's baseline player. Find out from past drafts how many players of each position were drafted in the first 100 picks. Use the past three years' draft data and if anything weight the last year's draft heavier than the latter two years. In 2006, my WCOFF 100 picks were 10 QBs, 40 RBs, 40 WRs, and 10 TEs. This is a fairly standard draft order for the first 100 picks in a 12 team, PPR format starting 1 QB, 2 RBs, 3 WRs, 1 TE, 1 K, 1 Def and 1 Flex (R/W/T). So the baselines are 10 for QBs, 40 for RBs and WRs and 10 for TEs. Notice no Kickers or Defense are predicted to be drafted in the first 100 picks through pick 9.04.

98 Drafting QB tips

If a QB has a record-breaking season, do not expect him to follow that up with another record-breaking season. It just does not happen. Records are broken but rarely duplicated. If it was such a record that few could do it to begin with, why would you expect a QB to be able to do it again the next season? Maybe everything clicked into place for the record to be broken; like few injuries to the OL, and WRs, an easy schedule, perfect timing of a bye, etc. These things do not happen often, so don't bet the bank on a repeat.

The QB position is relatively deep since there is less demand for it. Most leagues only start 1 QB. In a 12-team league this means that after all of the teams draft their starter and backup, there are still 8 more QBs left. Some teams may draft a third QB. But there will still be starters on the free agency list. Wait to draft your QB1 but then do not wait too long on your QB2. **Two good QBs can be better than one great QB and a low backup, if their matchups can be played well enough.** Paying too high a price for a QB (picking in the first 3 rounds) who will ultimately not be that far away from the QB10 is too much of a hurdle to overcome.

Most of the top QBs are not worth the high draft picks you pay for them. You can get some real steals in the late rounds of the draft, assuming you are not in a 14- or 16-team league or have some "start two QBs" rule, etc. You can wait on drafting a QB and still get one as good (if not better) than the one you passed on. (Wait till 8th or 9th round.) Studies have shown that if you wait to draft your QB and end up with QB5+QB19, you sacrifice 12% of the possible QB1+QB8 points. In other words, you lose 12% of the FPs at your QB position, but hopefully you make that up in the higher draft picks you have to devote to other positions. Waiting till everyone else has their QB then grabbing both of yours, QB12 and QB13, costs you very little more. Waiting until everyone has their QB and about half have a backup (Q18/19) and then getting your one QB costs you about twice as much. Three QBs do not offer more points than any of the two QB combos, so drafting three QBs is not worth it unless you are in a start two QBs league. **The best strategy is to wait and get the 10th-12th best QB and pair them up with another QB thereafter.**

Top 10 QBs tend to be 6' 4"- 6' 5" and weigh 225 lbs. QBs are more likely to rush for lots of yards and TDs in the first five years of their career. After that the wear and tear and sense of survival takes over. QBs tend to bloom at 26 or 27 years old, or four or five years into their career; about the time when they stop rushing so much and stay in the pocket. Evaluate young QBs by when they throw on 3rd and long (5 yards or more). Do they complete their passes? That will tell you something about how well they are going to do in the future in the NFL. If they do not complete them then they will not be in the NFL for very long. Finally, stay away from rookies and even second year QBs, who do not generally fair too well.

Injury affects this position more than you think. Most QBs miss a few games during the year (P. Manning, knock on wood, is one of the few exceptions to this rule).

Things to watch: Who is he throwing it to? How is the offensive line? What is his defense like (will he get the ball back a lot)?

99 Drafting RB tips

Remember, this is *your* franchise. Watch to see if he is an every down running back or just plays on 1st and 2nd downs. Does he get the goal line carries or does he have some vulture waiting to snatch those TDs from him? Does he catch balls well out of the backfield (B. Westbrook, Steven Jackson)? Is he stable on and off the field? Does he have a good potent offense (Indianapolis, New England) or does the team always find itself behind at halftime (Detroit Lions, St Louis Rams)? What is his defense like?

RBs get hurt the most, so plan accordingly. Betting the ranch on one stud RB is not the best game plan because injury could strike him at any time. Goal line vultures will be worth something in TD-only leagues, but not much beyond that. Avoid the RBBC. Injuries are the most common cause of an RBBC approach. Don't be too afraid of a rookie RB because they can learn their position more quickly than any other scoring position in the NFL. Do, however, watch the inevitable rookie hype (hint: overpriced). Historically, less than 50% of the top 3 RBs have repeated in the next year.

The typical Top 10 RBs are usually around 5' 11" and 220 lbs. Avoid RBs over 30 as most RBs who make it to their 10th year do not do as well. (Tiki Barber and John Riggins were the exceptions). RBs can be power-oriented (run-you-over type backs) or cutback runners. Big RBs that do not share time can be traded early, before they get dinged up, as they will start to falter in the second half of the season. Big RBs who share time should be saved for the stretch run as they tend to do better in the second half. RBs that are involved in the passing game tend to do as well, if not better, in the second half of the season. Rookie RBs tend to outperform in the second half of the season as well.

100 Drafting WR tips

After the first 10 or 12 WRs you lose all hope of consistent production for your money. Look for a great QB and the consistency that only the Top 10 QBs can provide. The next thirty WRs are anyone's guess and can be had for about the same amount, depending on who is making up the cheat sheets. Usually it takes 2-3 years in the NFL for players to get comfortable at this position and one year to learn a new team's system. WRs tend to break out in their 2nd or 3rd year. WRs tend to drop out of the Top 10 in their 7th or 8th year. The Top 10 WRs tend to be 6' or taller and 200 lbs. They are generally not as tall as TEs, but recently tall WRs have become stars.

What kind of WR? There are two types of WRs, speed and possession. Possession receivers do not have the speed to get open deep but are surer-handed. They are the ones crossing the middle of the field, getting lots of receptions and some yardage but not as many TDs. Generally speaking, the older a receiver the more he becomes a possession receiver and must learn to find the seams in a defense and "sit down" in a scheme to catch the underneath balls. The speed (or long ball or TD) WR will stretch the field and go deep more often, thus he will have more TDs and longer yardage TDs. They will generally be the younger WRs.

101 Drafting TE tips

Use the same criteria and time to learn the systems as WR in the tip above. The top ranked TEs perform consistently and prove more valuable. Expect them to go in the 3rd-5th rounds. Only a few top TEs are around after Top 5; more choices now at 6-10 TE. After that, wait. There is no reason to reach for back-up TEs. The drop off from the top 5 to top 15 is huge. You either get one of the big names or not. There is no reason to go fishing for a TE#2 until the late rounds. I mean last five, especially if you have to get a couple of kickers and defenses. Look for the same attributes as a backup WR. Make sure he is a pass-catching TE and not a primarily blocking TE, and look for a 2-4th year player who may break out.

102 Drafting K tips

Look for a kicker who has the same coaches and players, especially ones who have done well in the past but slipped in the rankings last year due to a key injury to themselves or a QB, RB, WR or TE on their team. Kickers on teams with a high amount of TDs the previous year are a good bet to kick more FGs this year (assuming the same QB). Regression to the mean should give the kicker more FG attempts. Finally, focus on kickers on teams with good defenses. This means they are in the game until the end and may have more opportunities to score.

103 Drafting Def tips

Watch out for Super Bowl (SB) champs. They usually have a crosshair on their back and everyone prepares well for them. Not to mention the fact that the defensive players get to go to more dinners and eat way too many meals and end up weighing more than their lean and trim pre-SB weight. A SB win equals a decline in the defense the following year. Injuries and losses to FA can also hurt a defense and make it lose some performance year to year. Know your scoring rules. Some award points for turnovers (TO) only, others for yardage allowed or points allowed. Remember special team (ST) points from KO and punt returns. Teams are lucky to have even one kickoff or punt returned for a TD. Look for that special playmaker that can make a difference (Devin Hester– Chicago).

Team defenses are usually taken in the latter part of the draft, especially if scoring is based on unpredictable TDs and turnovers, but if your league uses yardage and/or points allowed for team defenses, then this may move their draft spot up some. Most team defenses will score between 2-4 TDs on defense. In fact, many times a fumble occurs on a sack and many fumbles returned for TDs come from sacks, so you can see that the more times an opposing offense is throwing, the more likely good things will occur for your defense. So look for defenses that have offenses that score often. Good defenses are often a product of a great offense and a favorable schedule. But know your scoring rules. If your league gives negative points for yardage or points allowed, then this type of defense may not be good, since they will be giving up plenty of yards in their prevent defense and may even allow some garbage points at the end of the game. If your league only penalizes defenses that allow 35 or more points, then you are safe with this type of defense.

Finally, on backup defenses - don't. If you can get by with just one defense, do it. If not, try to get a backup with favorable matchups when your main DEF is on a bye. Most defensive points come from plays that are pass oriented. Points come from sacks, interceptions, safeties and TDs from INT returns, all of which happen when the offense attempts to pass. Other points such as fumbles for TDs are less rare.

104 IDP tips

IDP is rarely talked about in the print media but here are a few tips for IDP leagues. Use VBD to determine when to start drafting IDP. Just like VDP with QBs, RBs, etc., use VDP with Defensive Linemen (DLs), Linebackers (LBs) and Defensive Backs (DBs). That way you can compare a LB's worth to a WRs.

There are lots of IDP on the waiver wire, so do not forget to factor in supply and demand into VBD (See Appenidx B).

Look for "bend but don't break" defenses, not great defenses. The great defenses (example BALT) force so many "three downs and a punt" scenarios that they do not get lots of chances for tackles and turnovers. NE, on the other hand, has a "bend but don't break" attitude and they stay on the field more often. On the field more, means more chances for an IDP to score points. Another factor will be an offense that is not good, thus giving the ball back and putting their defense on the field again. In fact, having a great rush defense actually hurts the defense since that will force the other team to pass, in which case they usually move quickly or kick it away. Great defenses (especially great rush defenses) are a hindrance to great IDPs.

Forget the hype. The media loves to focus on the sack leaders. Know your FP projections and do not bite off on the big names but little IDP producers. (If your league does not require DL then go with LBs almost exclusively). The guy who tackles well is the one you want, not the one that show boats after a sack or INT and gets all the ESPN highlight time. Ignore the INT and fumbles recovered stat. They are hard to predict and there is not much difference between the leader and the #25 guy. **Look at solo tackles. They are the bread and butter of IDP scoring**.

105 Drafting IDP tips

Where would you draft an IDP? The answer is, as with many things, "it depends." In this case it depends on your scoring system. Does it award points for tackles, assists, turnovers and sacks? If so, then IDPs are going to be more valuable than if they were only awarded points based on sacks and turnovers. Remember there are lots of tackles and assists in every game. Tackles are the equivalent of yardage for IDPs. As a ROT, the fewer yards rewarded to skill players, the more valuable IDPs become; if your league awards 1 point for every 10 yards and 1 point for every tackle, then IDPs are worth about the same as

TEs and Ks. If your league only gives 1 point for every 25 yards and 1 point for a tackle, then IDPs become more valuable; on par with WRs. In this case, the top DL or LB may go as early as the 4th round. Most owners usually give them some thought after the starting RBs and WRs are gone. IDPs will fight with backup RBs and WRs for draft slots; usually rounds 6-8 if tackles and assists are rewarded. The problem with IDPs is there are so many of them compared with RBs and WRs. If your league has no scoring for assists and a minimal reward for tackles, then IDPs will start to be drafted toward the end of the WRs, but before K and most of the TEs (note there will be no DEF/ST to draft in an IDP league). IDPs will not supplant the offensive skill players except most TEs and they will be more valuable than the dreaded kicker.

Know the defensive schemes employed by the defensive units and the role the players will have in that scheme. **However, because there is so much depth at IDP and the differences between #10 and #40 at any position is less than the offensive skill positions, generally it will pay off to wait before drafting an IDP.** Get both starting RBs and WRs (if 3, get 3); then and only then think about IDPs. If the Top 5 at all the IDPs are gone (especially LB) then wait some more. Get your backup RB, WR and starting QB and TE, then in round 10 or 11 start to look at IDPs. Think TEs and kickers here. If you don't get a top one, then don't bother early.

Once you start to lessen the number of IDPs remaining after the draft, then those drafted will become more valuable. So the more IDP players, the more valuable they will be, but even in leagues that start 10 or more IDP players, offense will still be king. Why? Say you are in a 12-team IDP league that starts 11 IDP players (4 DL, 3LB, 4 DB) just like the NFL. Having 11 starters plus 11 backups equals 22 IDP players per team, times 12 teams = 264 players drafted. But remember, there are 11 players on 32 teams that start (not counting part-time players), so 352 IDPs (see Appendix B Supply and Demand of Fantasy Positions) in the NFL are available. That means 88 players are still on the FA list after the draft is over.

Many owners are unfamiliar with IDPs. This may be because more TV highlights are offensive scoring plays or simply because your league only recently went to IDPs. In any case, many owners have a bias towards offensive players and/or defensive stars and thus they do not do their homework when it comes to IDPs. Your knowledge of them can be where you set yourself apart from the rest of the pack. Drafting starting IDPs while others are getting QB and WR backups can give you a significant advantage.

1) Go with offensive players (starters) first since they are less deep in players.
2) Top IDPs at each position will probably go in the middle rounds; other IDPs in the late rounds and the kicker will still go with the last pick.
3) Save room on the bench for backup offensive players since they are less available on the waiver wire.
4) Grab LBs, and lots of them, if your league does not weigh IDP stats against them.
5) Once you get a good IDP at a position, move on to the next position or get depth at offensive positions. **Depth is not a must at IDP because of supply and demand.**

106 Play hunches

Some experts are going to advise you to always draft according to ADP data and frankly, that is a bunch of hooey. Go with your gut and play your hunches. There is nothing worse than wanting to draft a sleeper and waiting until the next round to draft him because his ADP says 13.11 and you have pick 12.10 and 13.3. Then the owner next to you with the 13.2 pick drafts your player. As sure as the sun sets in the west, that sleeper is going to have a glorious season for your opponent and probably in the irony of ironies, will end up beating you in the playoffs thanks to that sleeper's game-breaking performance. All because you did not want to pull the trigger in the 12th round on him and instead opted to grab your back up TE. If you have that strong of a feeling for the player, ADP be damned, draft him. If he is supposed to last till the 14th, grab him in the 13th. If other players you have targeted are going a round earlier than their ADP, learn the lesson and grab them two rounds before the ADP says. The bottom line is to use your instinct, and if others agree with you in a sleeper or two, then they will target them early as well. So be prepared to draft before the ADP says to and go with your gut on occasion.

107 Blocking/Around the corner

Blocking is drafting the next best player at a position your opponent needs. Blocking can occur when you suspect another owner after you needs to take a player and you can intervene and take them instead; hence, you block them from getting their player or position filled. Usually this occurs at the 3 or 4 position or 9 or 10 position in 12-team serpentine drafts; thus taking advantage of a wrap around pick or "going around the corner". If you have the 2nd, 3rd or 4th pick or the 9th, 10th or 11th pick, you can look at an opponent's needs/trends and get more value for your picks by choosing players they need, before they do. That is assuming that you need the player as well. If you have a choice between a QB and a WR and you cannot decide which to take, look at what your opponent needs. For example, you have the 10th pick of the draft; the owner with the 11th pick already has his QB, but the 12th spot does not. There is only one QB left in the good tier (top 15 QBs); if you take the QB that blocks the other owner from getting a decent QB. You have blocked him out of the good QB market. This tip is also known as "boxing out."

The Wrap Around or "Around the corner" pick involves picking before a team owner and then picking again shortly thereafter. This happens when you have the second, third or fourth pick or the 9th, 10th or 11th pick in a 12-team serpentine draft. The closer you are to the corner (last pick), the easier it is to make this tip work. If you are debating between a RB and a WR and you know there are two players in each tier you would like to draft, what do you do? First, determine how many players can be drafted before your next pick comes up "around the corner". If you are drafting 10th, then four picks will occur before your next pick. So if you choose wrong, the other player will not be available. Here is where being on the end comes in handy. You can play the other owners. If one owner is loaded with RBs and does not need another RB, then you should draft the WR because the odds are better that the other owner will not take both of the remaining RBs. By looking at what the other owners are likely to draft, you can calculate the smarter draft choice for your team. Remember the farther you are away from the corner (end or beginning of the draft order) the harder it is to employ this tip effectively. Fellow owners will not always draft logically either but it sure is better than not using it at all. I wish I had ten dollars for every instance where an owner on the corner did not take advantage of the wrap around situation.

108 Draft Smart

Use the draft tracker (Tip #73) to "see the forest for the trees." Use this information to make better draft decisions. If after looking at the tracker, you see that all of the other teams have their starting QB after 8 rounds, do not draft your starting QB next round as planned. You can afford to wait a round or two since the other owners are less likely to grab a QB2 early. So, if you had the 4th pick in the 9th round, wait and use it for another critical position, and then grab your QB in the 10th round as the draft makes its way back up to you.

Another example of "smart drafting" is taking a player if you see that other owners ahead of you are deficient in that position. If you have the 7th pick (6.07) and you see that every owner after you has yet to draft their TE (they will pick 12 players before you get another chance to pick), smart drafting may be to grab a decent TE now before the run starts. You may even be able to start the TE run.

Likewise, if 9 of the other 11 teams have a TE and you have 3 left in your tier on the cheat sheets, do not go after TE next. If there are three available and only two other teams need a TE1, you can wait a long time on the TE1 position and focus on other areas. At the worst, the other two teams needing a TE1 will take two off the tier and then you can grab the last tier TE before a team gets greedy and drafts their TE2.

109 Early rounds

What are the early rounds? In a 20 round league, rounds 1-7 are early. Rounds 1-3 should be scripted. You should know pretty well which three players you will have after these rounds. If you know your draft position and the ADP and the other owners' tendencies, then you should have a very good idea who will fall to you in these early rounds. Two RBs in the first three rounds is almost a given, depending on the league scoring/starter rules.

Round 1: RB unless you have a later draft pick and want to grab a stud WR. You should know who you want. Do not sweat your first round pick. It will probably not break you one way or the other unless you take a risk. Do not take a risk! Focus on having a good overall draft. Concentrate on picks 2-XX.
Round 2: Most likely RB, especially if you can start more than two RBs (i.e. through a flex option); if you can get a top WR and there are still RBs in your tier available next time, then go with a top WR (i.e late 2nd round pick). RB or WR, whichever you did not take with first pick, is a great generic strategy.
Round 3: Depends on whom you took with picks 1 and 2. Do not be locked into certain positions. Go with whom you need and who is the best value.
Rounds 4-7: Focus on what others have done and need. If everyone has a QB by now, you can afford to wait on your QB so look to a top TE or whoever is the best value on the board. Stock

up on RB and WR talent. Start a run on a position before anyone else does (as long as it is not a K or DEF).

Round 7: If you only have two RBs and two WRs by now (i.e. took a QB and TE too), get a third RB and WR soon.

Overall: Two WRs in the first 6 rounds. Do not get too many WRs since they have so much depth, unless you are in a start three WR and flex league, in which case three WRs in the first 6 rounds is a must. Three RBs and three WRs by round 6 is a good generic strategy. Historically there are 1-2 elite QBs and TEs but grabbing one before round 3 is probably a reach. The higher draft pick you use on any QB1 or TE1, the less value you get from the player. In other words, if you use a high draft pick on them they had better produce as expected, and if they do not produce, you will be hurt.

110 Middle Rounds

Go for QB in round 7 or 8 and QB2 soon thereafter. This will start a run on QB2s and can buy you some time. Draft for depth at RB and WR. Look for a starting TE if you do not have one by now. Avoid K and DEF (there will be runs on them in later rounds 10+). Get a HC for RB1 if not already taken.

Rounds 8-10: Add depth or finish out lineups? Best available players? Look for breakout candidates.

Rounds 11-13: Handcuffs, catch-up with RB or WR (by now should have 2 QBs, 4-6 RBs, 4-6 WRs, 1 TE).

Round 14: Think about K or DEF if top one on board with late bye week.

111 Late rounds

Late round advice is to take K1 and DEF1 with the last picks of the draft or a round earlier. Notice only 1 K and DEF, not two if allowed. Get your TE2 in a bye week different from TE1, K1 and DEF1 if you are not getting a K2 or DEF2. Look for sleepers and HCs if needed. The number of sleepers increases if you decide to forgo TE2, K2 or DEF2. Not drafting one or more of these will give you more room to grab another sleeper pick. Again, sleepers should be RB or WR.

Rounds 15-17: HC, bye week fill-ins, players with potential (sleepers).

Rounds 18-19: K or DEF if not already taken or K2 and DEF2 if required by rules.

So your final rosters will either be 2-3 QBs, 5-7 RBs, 5-7 WRs, 2 TEs, 2 Ks, 2 DEFs or 2 QBs, 6-8 RBs, 6-8 WRs, 1 TE, 1 K, 1 DEF or somewhere in between.

Personally, I think fewer TEs, Ks and DEFs and thus more RBs and WRs gives you the better team

112 Avoid groupthink

What is groupthink? It is when members of a group come to a consensus without really analyzing (thinking about) the data themselves. Sometimes groupthink occurs because members are too lazy to test the data. Other times it occurs to avoid conflict when members actually disagree. In the fantasy football community, all too many times it happens to avoid being seen as foolish or out of step with the community. Too many times the publications that promise rankings and projections do not really go out on a limb and provide you with anything new. Instead, they take last years stars, prorate for injuries and then sprinkle in some rookies. Shake well and you have a cookie cutter forecast that takes no chances and gives no advantages.

   Fantasy Football Almanac: The Essential Fantasy Football Reference Guide avoids groupthink by voicing my opinions regardless of how wacky or outrageous they may be. In 2008 when many had Derek Anderson and Joseph Addai as their poster children, I went with Aaron Rodgers and Ronnie Brown. Do not get me wrong, I miss on a few observations too (Larry Johnson in 2008 stands out), but I am willing to call it like it is, versus being afraid to be seen "missing one" on occasion.

   It seems that every year the same magazines and websites all have a consensus top 10 or close to that. Try and avoid falling into their trap of this is what will happen. Think outside the box and make your own observations. Look for publications that take a chance. Sure, they will miss on occasion, but you will find more gold searching on your own then you will in a stream full of others.

113 Take some chances with deep sleeper versus Vets

   It is the 15th round and you need to add your 7th WR. Your choice is the 10-year veteran who always puts up 45 catches, 500 yards and 4 TDs (119 fantasy points) or the 2nd year WR who played sparingly in his rookie season but showed some brilliance. Always go with the sleeper in the late rounds. Go with the player that has the highest upside potential. The chances are good that the reliable vet will not improve on his normal statistics. If anything he is more likely to go down as age, loss of a step and injuries take their toll. The younger player has lots of upside. He could start and really make a name for himself. Or he could start and flop. Nevertheless, either way at least he had a chance to really help your fantasy team.

   The vet provides no value. What are the chances that he will crack your roster? He is the 7th WR on your squad. Assuming it is a start 3 WR and play one as a flex if needed, that means at the most 4 WRs start each week. Factor in one out due to injury and one out due to a bye week and he still may never see the starting lineup. Yes, he provides a dependable three catch, 30 yard Sunday every week but that is not enough to help your team. Even if he does have a break out game, that is more than likely the exception rather than the norm. You are far better off taking a long shot on the sleeper than keeping dependable veterans as the last options at RB or WR.

114 Evaluate After the draft

The first thing you need to do after the draft is analyze how you did. Take stock of your team and evaluate how the draft went, based on your plan. Critique yourself immediately after the draft and write down any lessons learned so that you can implement them before your next draft. Heck, write the notes on the inside cover of this book, because if you are like me you have yellow post-it notes everywhere, except where you need them when you need them.

Ask yourself these critical questions.

Do I have any bye week issues? Is more than one starter on a bye week at the same time; if so did I try to get more on that same week to minimize the damage to that one week? If I do have bye week issues, can my backups cover adequately or do I need to add someone in free agency because I have no players that week?

Did I handcuff my RB1 or RB2? Is the handcuff player available in free agency and would that be cheap insurance now? Do I need to (is he a worthy handcuff (see Tip # 63)?

What are my teams' strengths and weaknesses? How can I improve in weak areas?

Tally up how the draft went by position and round. So how many of each position were drafted each round and what did each owner do round by round? The draft tracker can tell you overall numbers of players drafted per position, but only the actual draft results can tell you how many went in the top 100 or how late owner #5 waited to draft his QB.

115 Risk versus reward

At every draft, you, as the owner, are doing a risk versus reward analysis. There are the studs who put up big numbers and who rarely have problems (injuries, suspensions, issues with coaches/teammates). Those players are easy; grab them early and often. Then there are the players who will not get enough playing time to score any real points anyway, so they are never drafted. Scratch them off the cheat sheet. Then there are the tough choices. Basically, you have the steady eddies who consistently put up average numbers without fail but who do not produce big games, and the talented players who are hot and cold or have problems that hinder their ability to produce like the studs.

How much risk should you be willing to take? In a league where there is a H2H playoff system, you should take less risk than a total points league. In the playoff league you just need to make the playoffs and then it is single elimination, so in essence it is a two-season league. First season is to make the playoffs and the second season is a do-or-die single elimination tournament. It will not matter whether you made it to the playoffs easily or just sneaked in. All teams start with a clean slate and now you have a 1 in 4 chance (usually 4 of 12 teams make a playoff format). In a total points league, everything matters. It is you versus 11 other teams fighting it out the entire season. Therefore, it makes sense to take on more risk to set your self apart from the pack in these types of leagues. **It is smarter to take less risk in the league where luck (playoffs and single elimination) is more of a factor. It is better to take more risk in the league where luck is less of a factor.**

In general, the larger the bench the more risk is rewarded. The smaller the bench spots the less risk is rewarded. If you have more "extra" players you can afford to take on more risk because if the sleepers do not pan out you have not lost anything. In smaller bench leagues that sleeper may be taking a spot from someone you need to fill-in one week, thus costing you points. Less choice means conservatism is rewarded. Refer to *Fantasy*

Football Guidebook: Your Comprehensive Guide to Playing Fantasy Football for a detailed explanation.

How you run your bench will also dictate how much risk you can handle. If I plan to use a rotation for DEF or K, I could take on more risk. If I drafted a DEF with a late bye week (say week 9), or planned to do a DEF by committee approach, where I simply added the best available defense in FA each week, then I would not need to use a bench spot for another defense. This "extra spot" could be used to take a chance on a sleeper RB or WR. **I could take on more risk with the style or strategy of how I ran my bench.**

So where do I take risks? In a playoff league with no carryovers, points or byes, and a small bench and no room to play bench strategies (rotating TE/K/DEF not an option due to mandatory minimum position numbers; aka must have two defenses on roster at all times), then I draft conservatively and take the chance that I can add/drop/trade or pick starters better than the other owners. If I am in a total fantasy points-only league with 10 bench spots, I will take on much more risk knowing that I have to go for broke to win the championship and I have lots of room to take chances on sleepers. Therefore, there are leagues where risk pays off and leagues where consistency pays off.

Chapter 6 Roster Management

116 Never bench studs

There are four types of players: studs, quality, fillers and duds. Generally, your studs will be your top 2 or 3 draft picks. Therefore, they will be your RB1 and WR1 and maybe RB2 or WR2 thus a Top 10 RB or WR and maybe a Top 5 QB. The quality players are your RB3 and WR3. The filler players are consistent players who can perform when faced with the correct match up. The duds are players who you start if you have to, but whom you do not count on too much. There is a reason why studs were drafted that high.

Adrian Peterson and Peyton Manning should never be benched unless they are on a bye week or are hurt and thus doubtful or out for the game (or unless they lose their job; fat chance). Why? Simple – they are your highest scoring players (that is why you drafted them so high in the first place) and thus they will score the most for you over the season. Do not worry about matchups. They are going to provide you big points if you start them week in and week out. Start them and forget about them. The minute you bench one because he is playing against the best defense is the minute he scores three TDs and has a career high day. Trying to time their big games is like trying to time the stock market. DON'T DO IT.

If the stud has a slow start or a game or two below average, rest assured that he will return to the mean eventually. You just do not want to have him on your bench when he does. If you try to time the big games and the bad games, you will be burned more times than you win, so start them no matter what. Do not over analyze the matchups. You will not lose sleep by starting your stud(s) and then one of them has an off day. You will lose sleep if you bench AP for Reuben Droughns and AP scores four TDs.

Never bench your stud players, or as Erik Barmack and Max Handelman state as their In-season Fantasy Football Motto

#1 "Always start your studs." Incidentally, their book **Why Fantasy Football Matters (And our lives do not)** has an excellent diatribe about "expert advice and analysis." I read it at least twice a year when I get frustrated answering these types of mailbag questions. Speaking of funny books about fantasy football; Mark St. Amant's **Committed: Confessions of a Fantasy Football Junkie** is my all time favorite. It is part Bill Bryson, Bill Cosby and every day fantasy footballer. A must read. But I digress.

117 Use Las Vegas to help with start/bench decisions

Always start your studs. Check. Now what, how do you decide which of the other players should start? I suggest you use the Las Vegas bookies to help you out, especially for the lesser player (WR, K, and DEF) decisions. If you have a choice between two kickers, who do you take? First look at the Las Vegas odds for both games they are playing. Jason Elam is one kicker as ATL plays Oakland. The other kicker is David Akers as Philadelphia plays Washington. Look at the over/under and then who is favored in both games.

ATL -3 Oak +3 O/U 37

Phil -7 Wash +7 O/U 47

For those unfamiliar with these terms, Atlanta is favored to win by 3 points. Philadelphia is favored to win by 7 points. The over/under refers to how many total points (TPs) both teams are expected to score in the game. The higher the over/under, the higher scoring is expected. If a player's team is in a higher scoring game and they are favored by a large margin, then Las Vegas expects their team to score a lot.

The bookies expect Atlanta to win 20-17 and expect Philadelphia to win 27-20. David Akers should have one more extra point than Jason Elam. Obviously, the bookies do not know exactly what will happen but they do odds for a living and thus the over/under should be quite accurate. The over/under says that they expect Philadelphia to score more points than Denver because Philadelphia is favored by more points and the over/under is higher for their game. All else being equal, go with Akers today. If you need to decide between two equal players who will just be a bye week fill-in, choose the player scheduled to play in the higher scoring game (higher over/under score). Be sure to look at the amount a favored team is predicted to win by. There may be instances when a lower over/under game will provide a higher team score because of the lopsidedness of the predicted victory margin; for more on this subject see Stephen Nover's book, *Winning Fantasy Football.* Nover is a sports betting professor at UNLV (how can I get that job?), who touches on the Las Vegas odds and their relationship to fantasy football in his book, *Winning Fantasy Football.*

Another feature to assist you in whom to start is the bookies NFL Propositions (also known as Props) on individual players and their statistics for the game. This usually comes in the form of an over/under on performance factors such as receptions, rushing yards, receiving yards, passing yards or TDs or the likeli-hood thereof. If Vegas has the over/under for Eli Manning at 219.5 yards passing, that is a great place to start your expectations. Realize that props come out and the odds will change as more information becomes available. So the closer you are to game time, the more accurate the prop. Weather cannot be adequately predicted 5 days out so that is usually the biggest wildcard, especially in December. Look at several sites and compare the odds, as there is some movement in both directions between sites.

118 Look at matchups

Therefore, you have started your studs (RB1 and WR1 and maybe RB2). You looked at the Vegas odds and decided which kicker and TE to start, but your choice at QB is too tight. What else can you use? Look at the matchup; see which defense they both face this week. Compare each defense's rushing yardage allowed; passing yardage allowed and points allowed. If the defense is good versus the run and their offense gets out in front a lot, then opponents (your QB) will be passing more against that defense and if they run-prevent a lot in the fourth quarter, their passing yardage may be higher than most. Tough defenses (especially if they face each other) tend to produce a physical game, which leads to turnovers (INTs), penalties and low scores. If faced with two QBs who should do about the same, start the one playing the easier defense, as he is more likely to have a great game, as opposed to the one facing the better defense.

Many of the fantasy football websites provide strength of schedule (SOS) information and some even go so far as to calculate projected fantasy points allowed by defenses per position. For example, the Minnesota Vikings have allowed TEs an average of 5 catches, 65 yards and .8 TDs this season so TE X should have 6 catches, 75 yards and a TD this week. Just remember garbage in and garbage out. You usually get what you pay for with those sites.

119 Field conditions

This does not address weather conditions. We will get into that later (tip # 120). This is simply the condition of some of the playing fields in the league and their tendencies. For example, Giants Stadium, which hosts both the NY Giants and NY Jets (on differing weeks, of course) is known for cold, strong, nasty swirling winds which tend to hurt QB numbers. Chicago is another place where winds hurt QBs, and to some extent kickers, but the kicking problem is due to proximity to water. The wind and water effect (heavier air) leads to the ball not going as far.

Pittsburgh's Heinz Field, Chicago's Soldier Field and
Jacksonville's Alltel Stadium are the worst to kick from due to
their proximity to water. Heinz Field kickers hate it. Swirling
winds, one end enclosed, one end open, a dirt field and the fact
that many other football teams use it ensures that it is a rough
surface. The cold of Soldier Field does not help either. A football
only weighs 1.4 pounds so imagine what a strong wind can do to a
kicker's accuracy. Denver is good because the high altitude makes
the ball go further. Miami is difficult because it can be windy and,
here is the important part, because of the infield dirt. Early in the
season if football overlaps with baseball (Florida Marlins), then
the infield dirt is a poor surface to have to kick off of. Surprise,
surprise; domes are the best places to kick from.

Be leery of kickers in Chicago, Pittsburgh, Jacksonville or Miami
and QBs in New York or Chicago.

120 Weather (WX) conditions

          Before you read anymore, do yourself a big favor and
bookmark the weather channel NFL weather page as a favorite.
Go to www.weatherchannel.com and select the tab "In Season"
and then "National Football League." You can now see the
temperatures and weather for game time. If you click on the
game, you will see a detailed forecast. Use this as a reference tool.
          Winds will affect QBs, WRs and kickers. Swirling winds are
the worst. If it is a constant wind from the same direction, QBs
and kickers can compensate, but when the wind changes direction
and speed frequently, all bets are off; unless your defense is
playing there, then that is a good thing! Of course, domes
neutralize whatever the outside weather is like.
          Do not be too worried about snow. Many WRs love snow
because they know where they are going and can use it to their
advantage. WRs will also slip less. They can adjust a bit. The
defensive player will slip more because he is reacting and does not
know where he is going. However, be wary of heavy snow since

this will affect the ability of the QBs and kickers to put the ball a long way down field.

Rain is the most difficult weather condition to take into account. Joe Theisman says that rain affects some quarterbacks and does not affect others. He says he was not bothered by rain because of where he gripped the ball. The balls are taken in and out and dried off after plays and receivers and QBs try to keep their hands dry. The effect it has on vision is probably most dramatic, as a heavy downpour limits down field views.

Cold weather can affect an entire team, especially if it is a dome team or a warm weather team traveling to a road site that has particularly cold weather. This effect usually becomes more prevalent in mid to late November and throughout December. Good examples are Miami and Jacksonville when they go on the road in December. Cold weather (and I mean really cold weather) is great for RBs, especially those who will get many carries in the second half. By then, the RBs are warming up and the defenders are wearing down. Cold is especially good if it is a night game because it gets colder as the game goes on. Defenders start to tackle poorly due to the cold and the RB gets better and better.

WIND = QB, WR and K problems

SNOW = Good for WRs and QBs but not heavy snow which affects downfield visibility
COLD = Bad news for dome teams and warm weather teams when on the road, great for RBs

Outdoor stadiums in northern climates: Buffalo, Chicago, Cincinnati, Cleveland, Denver, Green Bay, New England, New York (Giants and Jets), Philadelphia, Pittsburgh, Seattle

One example comes from 2008 when in week 16 Kurt Warner traveled to New England with a 285 yard/1.73 TD average per game. Prior to this game, he had 4,289 yards and 26

TDs for the season. But in the game he was 6 of 18 for 30 yards (no TDs or INTs). Dave Gerczak took advantage of this to become the 2008 NFFC $100,000 Champion (see Foreword). Why the big difference? Well for one it was against NE at Foxboro. However, it was also very cold and snowing heavily. Weather can change a player's statistics quickly.

121 Injuries - Know who to believe

The NFL releases weekly injury reports but that information comes from the team. Injury reports are fluid lists. They change from Wednesday to Friday to Saturday to Sunday morning to game time, so be wary of some of the information. Some coaches may list an injury and say it is more serious than it is, hoping his opponents do not plan for that player. Others underestimate the injury so that opponents waste time game-planning for that player. You need to know the coaches and the players they are talking about. Laveranues Cole plays and Todd Heap plays. Tennessee Titans head coach Jeff Fisher has a habit of listing every player who is "dinged up" as questionable or out every week. There is a big difference between a player having an injury and whether that player plays the game. Avoid NFL sites for this information and find a good source that can tell you reliably what will happen.

The NFL has four terms it asks coaches to use in categorizing injuries. They are PROBABLE, which means the player has a 75% chance of playing. QUESTIONABLE, which means he has a 50% chance of playing. DOUBTFUL, which means (you guessed it) he has a 25% chance of playing that week. The last term is OUT and that means he will not play that week. Caveat: there have been a few rare instances where a player is listed as OUT but played anyway. Teams and coaches can get into big trouble if this happens because they are required to provide information to the betting public and bad information may alter the odds in one way or another. So if a team says a player is

"OUT," you can trust them on that. This is not to say that you should believe the other three terms without question.

Questionable players play in about 60% of their games (a little more than the 50 percent advertised by the NFL). On average, even if your player does play when his status is questionable, his performance will suffer. NOTE: There are exceptions, but on average, his stats will suffer if listed as questionable. What is the drop in stats? If he is a QB expect fewer TDs but about the same yardage. If a RB or WR, expect half as many TDs and a drop in yardage. Players listed on the injury report in previous weeks and then downgraded to "questionable" are not good starters. Nor are players who do not practice on Thursday or Friday; unless they are someone like T. Owens or P. Buress. How a player handles the days after the game is just as important as the game itself with regards to injuries.

Note what decisions you have made and keep them handy while watching the pre-game shows, so you know if you need to make any adjustments based on injury upgrades or downgrades. CBS, Fox and ESPN all have a ticker on their pre-game shows that tells the weather and injury status for each of the games

122 Do not start "doubtful" or "out" players.

It is very simple, straightforward advice. This is not to say that occasionally your stud will be listed as doubtful and then go on to score a zillion points on your bench. Such is life. More often than not though he will not play or will play to such a limited or injury plagued degree that he is not worth starting. If I play a doubtful player it is because he is a stud who has been upgraded at game time and I have no other replacement. Questionable players should be started unless you have a good enough (equal) backup or a lesser player with a great matchup. Probable players should play unless you have an equal player that can replace them. Some players listed as probable do not play (DNP). I usually bench questionable players until I hear more on game day. Start them if you do not have an equal replacement. If your player is questionable and you have no replacement, then you can do a FA pickup; but don't drop the injured player necessarily (especially if he is a stud). Drop one of your sleepers who have not panned out.

123 Be careful starting "questionable players" in December

Injuries become even more significant in December when you are trying to reach the playoffs or win your championship in the playoffs. Players are more tired, have nagging injuries and are more likely to get hurt in December games. Do not take chances on injured players in December. Play it extra safe toward the end of the season as far as starting questionable players.

124 Track looks, touches and red zone touches

Looks are opportunities for pass catching. If a player has a pass thrown his way, the QB has given him a "look'. More "looks" mean either he is getting open or the QB has confidence in the player's ability to catch the ball. A touch is a catch or a carry if rushing. A high look to touch ratio means the player catches most of the balls thrown his way. This is a self-fulfilling prophesy, as the better pass catcher you are, the more looks you get, the more catches you make. Touches equate to chances to score. The more a RB carries the rock (and catches it), the greater the chance he will score a TD. The same applies to WRs and TEs. The more catches they have, the better chance of them scoring a TD for you.

Red Zone touches are catches within the opponents' 20-yard line. If you catch the ball there it is more likely to be a TD then if your player caught the ball within his own 20-yard line and had to run 80+ yards to the end zone. So the more red zone touches, the higher the chance for a TD. Red zone touches can be an indicator that the offense is trying to get him the ball in these goal line situations. If I have two equal players and one has more red zone touches-he gets the start over the other equal player.

125 Play the schedule

Look at the schedule and use it to help you make those tough start/bench decisions. Often there will be a reason for poor performance. Thursday night games tend to be sloppy, poor performance affairs. So defenses tend to be better than average and QBs not so much. Why? It takes until Friday to recover from Sunday games normally. That recovery time is shortened by three days if you play on Thursday. Teams also have less time to prepare. Thus the offense has less time to figure out special plays against the defense. Defenses adapt to a shorter workweek better than the offense. The same logic applies for Thanksgiving (since it is played on Thursday) but even more so for the teams that play the first game. They have even less time to recover and prepare than if they played on Thursday night. The home team really does have a big advantage on a Thursday game simply because of no time lost to travel.

International games are worse in some regards, as teams have to fly to another continent and adjust to a far different time zone. Add in the extra media coverage, sightseeing, promotional duties and jetlag, and that gives you two tired teams. So the one international game (played in London every year recently) tends to be a defensive struggle. SD vs NO in 2008 proved the exception to the rule. Speaking of jetlag and travel, beware the dreaded west coast team flying to the east coast for their game. Most west coast teams have a difficult time traveling and adjusting to the time change. East coast teams seem to handle going west much better.

Finally, use nationally televised games as your final discriminator. If you have used all of the roster management tips listed in this book (Tip # 116-126) and still have two players equal; consider if they play on a nationally televised game. Start the one in the nationally televised game. They will have more incentive to highlight themselves to the country. These games have a little extra excitement and testosterone. It may just be the edge you need. Monday Night Football is the nirvana of nationally televised games. If you find yourself with a player on MNF at home, give him the advantage.

126 Use the message boards (MBs) for help, inspiration or just a sounding board

Some owners ignore the message board (MB) because they think it is nothing but a bunch of whiners who have too much time on their hands. Nothing could be farther from the truth. Usually these are the diehard fantasy footballers who use the MB to test the waters for start/bench decisions. If you want to avoid making a huge roster blunder, run it by the MB. Do not wait until the last second to post because the number of replies will be limited and most footballers are doing just what you are doing before kickoff; surfing the net for last minute injury updates. Instead start a MB entry on Friday night about your starting dilemma and then sit back and evaluate the responses.

Take everything with a grain of salt too. Some posters may try to sabotage you (especially if this is an upcoming draft question). Others may be less knowledgeable about the players than you. But overall, many of the replies will be well thought out, articulate explanations of what they think you should do and why. Often these discussions can lead to other topics, like who is the best RB or what was your biggest drafting mistake; overall good therapy for a dedicated fantasy footballer.

Chapter 7 Free Agency

127 Free Agency Blocking

Blocking is a tactic in which you grab a free agent player that your opponent needs, even though you do not need them. A perfect example occurs when Matt Forte goes down with an injury. He hurts his hand the previous week and then on Wednesday is declared out for the upcoming week. Your opponent this week is the owner of Matt Forte. If he has not handcuffed Matt Forte's backup, then you would be wise to grab Garrett Wolfe off the free agent list. This is beneficial to you in many ways. First, G. Wolfe may prove to be a good RB to start this week based on his matchup. Secondly, Matt Forte may be out for the rest of the season, in which case you just picked up another starting RB. Perhaps best of all, you have BLOCKED this week's opponent from picking up a serviceable RB. He will be cursing you when he sees that you have scooped up his backup even though you do not need him. This can prove to be a very successful strategy. The same thing can happen even if you do not want the backup. Say, for example, that P. Manning goes down for your opponent this week; perhaps J. Sorgi does not appeal to you as a good QB to have regardless of the status of P. Manning. In that case, you can still BLOCK your opponent by grabbing the best QB available on the free agent list. This prevents your opponent from getting the better backup, assuming he does not have a suitable backup on his bench. QB, RB and TE will usually be the positions for which this strategy works best. Other positions (WR and K) are too deep and defenses never have injuries that would force an entire defense to be unusable.

128 Have a FA watch list

Always have a "watch list" of at least three players from each position that you would add if you had an injury. Think about it this way: "If I could keep two more players at each position, who would I draft?" Perhaps they are sleepers that you want to pull the trigger on if they start to perform. Keep up with who is available and who was just released. When a team adds a player, check out whom they dropped and evaluate them for potential. Many times these are players who were drafted but have just not performed lately. Jump on them if there is a reason to expect a rebound. The players that are dropped most often, when a good FA or waiver wire player becomes available, are K2 and DEF2. Always be on the lookout to snag one of these kickers or defenses if they can help you. NOTE: Many websites will let you mark players as watch list; this makes it easy to keep tabs on them as the season progresses and allows you to delete players that others have added.

129 Use the odds to determine which FA to pick up short term

Use "Vegas" odds in determining which FA to pick up. You have narrowed down your FA pickups to two WRs. Which one will perform better this week? (Assuming this is just a stopgap substitution for a bye week WR or flex player.) Choices are J. Higgins (OAK) or S. Rice (MIN). The odds-makers say:
Example: OAK -3/GB +3 over/under 45 means the Vegas bookies expect Oakland to win 24-21.
Example: MIN +7/Den -7 over/under 35 means Denver is expected to win 21-14.
All other things being equal, go with Higgins and OAK. They are expected to score 10 more points than Minnesota, thus a greater chance for a TD for Higgins than Rice.

130 Use the upcoming schedule for Long Term (LT) Free Agents

Do they have favorable matchups? If a QB, look for weak pass defenses. If RB, look for weak rush defenses; for kickers look for poor defenses in general. A favorable DEF/ST would involve playing low scoring offenses, inexperienced QBs, etc.

131 Carry two kickers in the middle of November/End of Free Agency

Carry two kickers starting in the middle of November. At the very least get your spare kicker before the end of the free agency period, if there is an end. This makes sure you are covered in case of injury after the FA period ends. There is nothing worse than seeing your kicker pull a hamstring on a fake kick, only to be sidelined for the next 2-3 weeks and your playoff bound team becoming kicker-less. Another reason to do this is to cover yourself when the bad weather starts to affect games. If your K1 is playing outdoors in a swirling snowstorm, with a K2 at least you have other options.

132 Proactive not reactive in free agency

Lead, do not follow, in free agent transactions; plan for your bye weeks at least two weeks in advance. Try to be one-step ahead of the other owners. They will be thinking one week ahead. If you are looking for a WR or K that has a good matchup in two weeks, you are much more likely to get him than if you wait until one week away and have to compete with every other owner who is also looking for a bye week replacement player from that position.

133 Handcuff sooner rather than later

Handcuff your RB if he starts to get gimpy or if the head coach indicates a change may be forthcoming. You should handcuff him in the draft (Tip # 63), but if you didn't then, definitely handcuff him if your starter begins to come up a little lame at times. Nagging little injuries late in the game can be an indicator of problems ahead. The head coach making statements like "Rex Grossman is our man for now" may be an indication of things to change in the future. Read between the lines.

134 Don't just pickup - matchup

If looking for a bye week pickup, make sure he has a great matchup in the week you are going to use him. For example, you select P. Manning as your #1 QB and do not draft another QB due to Peyton's never missing a game. Peyton has his bye week in week 6 so you need to add a QB in week 4 (two weeks early; think ahead, beat the rest) that has a favorable matchup in week 6. Bypass a better overall QB for one that has the best matchup in week 6, which is the only week your backup will start.

135 One owner's woes are another's opportunity

A starter's injury can be your ticket to the acquisition of a great player. Look for injuries and grab the backup to the injured player, especially if it is a starting RB. What about an injury to your player? Your preparedness will determine the champs from the pretenders. Do you have the HC? Do you have a backup RB #3 to fill in? Can you trade away some bench depth to recover? If you do not have the HC, grab him immediately if your starter is out. Some will hesitate and begin to over analyze. "What if he does not start?" "What if he is not any good?" GRAB HIM NOW. If you wait, someone else will grab him to block you. He will definitely do better than your injured player who is out. If he does not start, then try to grab the guy who did start or make other plans for next week. But having a plan (grab his backup) is better than no plan at all. Don't forget to look to the M*A*S*H unit for stars who have injured themselves and are off the radar screen. Always keep in mind when they are scheduled to return. You may have to add them a week earlier to keep the other owners out. Remember to be cautious with them when returning from injuries, but many times a pickup in week 10 or 11 can turn into a jewel come playoff time.

136 Avoid 1 game wonders

There are some owners who will jump on a RB or WR who has a 100-yard game. Evaluate him but also look critically at his performance. Was he a first week wonder? Did he play because the star was banged up and could not play? Is he a new player on the team and this was just the beginning? Is he a RB who had three carries for 101 yards but one of those carries was a fourth quarter dash for 93 yards as the game ended?

137 Analyze their game history

You can usually use websites to sort players based on their stats. Look at FP scored, and then look at TDs and yardage. Look at catches for WR and carries for RB. A player with many catches/carries but few yards may mean less TDs down the road, but someone with lots of catches/carries and yards may be just around the corner from scoring on those big plays. Rookies who are getting more and more touches should be considered sleeper material. The longer you go into the season, the more you will need to look at game-by-game performances. As an example, it is week 10 and you are looking at a WR to replace an injured WR#2. A WR with four TDs, but all of them in week 2, is not as good a WR with only three TDs, one each from the last 3 games. What have you done for me lately?

Free Agent Acquisition Budget (FAAB) Tips

138 FAAB - Never bid in round numbers

Always use odd numbers, one over what you think the round number is you should bid. If you think $300 should be bid, than bid $301; if it is $250, than bid $251. You have more of a chance of tying with round number bids (200, 250, and 300). The extra dollar is to be different and prevent a tie.

139 Balance week 1 exuberance with week 3-5 maturity

The first few weeks are critical to finding and adding new players. Every year there is a surprise player who takes off in week 1 with a breakout game. In 2003, it was Anquan Boldin (AZ) and his 10 catch, 217 yard, 2 TD day (101-1377-8 for the season). In 2008 it was Eddie Royal (Denver) who had 9 catches, 146 yards and 1 TD (91-980-5 for the year). For every Boldin and Royal there are a Dante Rosario (CAR, TE). Rosario went 7-96-1 in week 1, but finished 18-209-1. Examine why a great week one performance occurred. Do not blow your entire free agent budget on a one-week wonder. Instead, balance your enthusiasm with why it happened. Is it likely to repeat? If so, try and get him after week 1 before others do. If it is not likely to repeat, wait and save your money for weeks 3-5 when teams are starting to show their true colors. **After week 4 you should know who is upwardly mobile and who is mired in mediocrity. That is the best time to invest those FAAB dollars.**

140 Keep track of bids and balances

Always know how much every owner has left in his FAAB. If you get down to week 10 and you have more than all the other owners, you can strategically limit your bids to just over what the maximum possible bid can be from the other owners, thus securing a player automatically. For instance, if you have $101 left and the only closest owner has $73. If you really want the player, a bid of $74 will guarantee you add him, since you have outbid everyone else. It would be stupid to bid more than $74 in this case because anything else would be wasting FAAB money.

Track how much others have spent on individuals and positions. If you notice that no owner has spent more than $5 on a kicker and you need one, then $6 is a pretty sure thing if you really wanted a specific kicker from the waiver wire. The real trick is to watch what others are bidding on WRs and QBs. RBs are so rare that they tend to be extravagant if one turns into a starter overnight unexpectedly and is still available through free agency. If you can, look at other similar leagues and see what their free agent acquisition amounts are for specific players and positions. Of course, a player's value can change from week to week and league to league. A backup RBs value increases exponentially when the starter comes up lame.

141 Always keep money for the end of the season

Injuries will happen. It would be a tragedy if both your kickers in the championship week came up hurt and all you needed was $1 to add another kicker, but you had no money left to spend. Even if you have the perfect team and tons of backups and cannot anticipate a need to add another player, you still want the option if needed. Another scenario may have you wanting to block a rival from adding a player needed due to injury.

142 Always plan for a maximum # of bids

By this I mean do not miss out on a player desperately needed simply because lots of other owners took the few players you bid on. If you need a bye week TE, K or Defense as a replacement, do not just put in two or three bids for that position. What if three other owners do the same, ask for the same Kickers, and outbid you. You could find yourself without a kicker for the week all because you were too lazy to submit a few extra "insurance" bids. Always put in more than enough bids to secure a position if all you really need is a warm body. For example, if I need a kicker just for the week I put in as many bids as there are teams. In a 12-team league I bid on 12 kickers, that way I can never miss out. I bid the most for who I really want and then put in the minimum amount for my "insurance" bids. These are to insure I get a kicker, no matter what.

143 Look at who needs what

Sometimes you can block another owner from getting a K or TE on a bye week if you have enough roster spots or pickups or free agency budget money. Usually this only occurs in 14 or 16-team leagues or leagues with large rosters. But if you do not plan for such a strategy, then when the opportunity presents itself you will not be ready to implement it. The first step to a successful block (if you see a rival needs a position player for the week (QB, TE, K or Defense; RB and WR are too deep with backups)) is knowing who needs what players for the week or weeks ahead.

Chapter 8 Psychology of fantasy football

144 Avoid using narrow sample sizes

Owners base broad predictions on narrow samples of data (the law of small numbers) when, in fact, they should use the law of large numbers. The law of large numbers states that only a large sampling of data can give an accurate picture of the information it is drawn from. When we add a player who has scored two TDs in the last three games, even though he is the #2 WR (on a team that does not pass well, and history shows has not done well at the WR#2 positions) we are using the law of small numbers. Try to use large samples of data to make predictions of the future. That is why three years' worth of statistics is what I recommend for AVT rankings (See Tip # 44).

145 Remember the past but objectively, not subjectively

If something is easy to remember, we tend to think it happens more often. Like hitting that sleeper pick, the rookie RB, or our boom/bust player's great games (versus his bust games). When we think of rookie superstars, everyone remembers Reggie Bush and Matt Forte. Both came into the league and started out on fire (Forte had 8 TDs and 63 catches his rookie season and Reggie had 8 TDs too, plus 2 in the playoffs). Therefore, they are easy to remember because of how well they did. However, that does not mean that many rookies do well in their first year, rather it is quite the opposite. Therefore, the easily remembered event leads us to take risky chances on rookies, when in fact only rookie RBs tend to do well and even then only 33 percent of the top rookie RBs perform well.

146 Pride in ownership

Losing feels worse than winning and we will do almost anything to prevent losing. Losing can mean a game or a player. Owners tend to hold on to poor performing players too long and trade/drop good players too soon. Why? We hate to admit a loss when we drop a player we drafted. If we drop a player we handpicked, we are admitting that we did not know what we were doing when we drafted, traded or added him. Likewise, if one of our players has done well lately, we have a tendency to trade him too soon so that we can acknowledge his accomplishments and bask in his glory.

147 Regression to the mean

We see trends where there are no trends. We don't realize regression to the mean. Chance alone dictates that an unusually good or bad event is usually followed by a more ordinary one. If a player has scored 10 TDs most of his career and is in the middle of the season with only 1 TD, unless he has been injured or has lost a key component to the offense (QB, RB, etc.), then that player should regress to the mean. By this I mean he should rebound with a higher than average number of TDs for the remainder of the season. Likewise, if a player has 6 TDs on average for the past four years and this year has 5 TDs in eight games, regression to the mean dictates that he will probably have less than the average number of TDs the remainder of the season. He may finish with seven or even eight TDs, but he probably will not continue with five more TDs in the next eight games. He may do just that, but the odds are against him due to regression to the mean, assuming all other variables (injuries, systems changes) stay the same. Tom Brady threw 50 TDs in 2007. The odds were against him having anywhere near that many in 2008 if he had stayed healthy. We tend to see trends and believe them (for example, 5 TDs in eight games, above) when there are no trends.

148 Familiarity bias

Players on "Homer" teams or players held by owners in previous years that did well will be drafted a round earlier than predicted. We have something in our subconscious that makes us hold onto them since we know them. Many owners will only remember the good or great performances by players on their team last year and thus overvalue them. Subjective memories lead us to over inflate known players. We know them like family and will do anything to get them back.

149 Sunk costs

Once we invest in a player or a theory, we tend to talk ourselves out of abandoning it because of the time or capital we have invested in it. The best reason not to draft a kicker early is that if he gets off to a slow start, you feel obligated to stick with him, rather than cutting him and going with a better option from FA. If you are not heavily invested in your kicker (high draft pick), then you are more likely to look at improving that position. The same goes for any highly drafted player. Owners will say, "I can't bench him, I drafted him too high."

150 Do not overreact

Most owners will overreact to both good and bad player news. This means they will sell a good player when he has had a few bad games and they will buy an average player after he has had a few good games. They are in effect, buying high and selling low. Take advantage of that. Know why you drafted a player and why you are dropping a player. Has anything changed with your initial analysis?

151 Think long-term not short-term

Do not worry about every yard or TD every week obsessively if you drafted them long-term (either for the entire year or several years if keeper league). Focus on how they have done at midseason or end of the season. You do not ask how much your house is worth every day, so don't worry about players every week. Studies show that owners who get wrapped up in analyzing their team each day get too consumed in the short-term statistics. (I think I'll bench AP this week since he plays at Baltimore. Instead, I will start Reuben Droughns at home versus Indianapolis.) At a minimum, wait for the first three weeks to unfold.

152 Look at the big picture

Try to see the forest for the trees. Don't panic because your #1 RB has not scored any TDs in the first four weeks. Look at your entire team, look at the league, and look at his NFL team. Maybe the first four weeks were low scoring statistically throughout the NFL. Maybe he played the toughest defenses on their schedule; maybe the key OT that helps make the holes for him was out and will be back soon. Don't rush to conclusions before looking at as much data as possible.

153 Do not over think

Use autopilot – Plug in the studs and leave them there. They are the studs because they will deliver stud-like returns. Randy Giminez in **Dominate Fantasy Football** puts it very simply. "If both of them or all {Website services}…are saying the exact same thing or very similar, do not question, just follow. Sometimes the more you think about a situation the more you'll shoot yourself in the foot". If you try to "time" the league and move studs in and out based on matchups, you are more likely to have your stud on the bench when he has a breakthrough day and vice versa. Constant tinkering produces poor results. Many teams would be better off without as many roster changes and add/drops. I have seen many owners who draft well and then only make changes to replace injured/suspended players; they do well because they avoid trying to time their performance and accept a good performance versus a great performance (with the risk of a below-average performance).

154 Never quit

Never abandon or give up on a team. Even if you are out of playoff contention (i.e. mathematically eliminated) continue to field the best team that you can. Turn in your best possible roster week in and week out. Doing that is the honorable thing but also the prudent option as well. Imagine, if at the end of the regular season, the commissioner declared one of the playoff teams ineligible due to some unforeseen reason (collusion, not paying entry fee, or just quitting, etc). You might still make those same playoffs that you thought were out of reach. Imagine another team getting in and you looking in from the outside, when, if you had not quit, you could have made it.

Chapter 9 Trade Tips

155 Use K and Def as sweeteners

The two easiest positions to add to a trade to sweeten the deal are kickers and defenses. They provide extra value at little cost to the trader. You can get another kicker or defense (top 5 excluded) from the waiver wire or maybe even one of your trading partners' kickers or defenses he does not want. Whatever it takes to get the trade approved. Of course, if you have a top 5 kicker or defense, they are worth more than most.

156 Look for add-ons

If you are going to drop the backup TE you have been carrying anyway once you acquire your trading partner's stud TE, then offer that TE as part of the trade. Some owners actually think that more players are a better trade, even though they will ultimately have to drop a player from their team if they get more players than they traded. Look for players he will have to drop to make room on his roster. If there is someone on his bench that you would rather have than allow going to the waiver wire, ask for them.

157 Watch the bye weeks in trade deals

Think about bye weeks for trades too; very simple but often unheeded advice. Watch out for bye weeks coming up and account for them in player value. Players A and B are equal in value. Player A has had his bye week, player B has his bye week coming up. Who would be the most valuable? Player A since he has all the games remaining as an asset, whereas player B will miss one week of the remaining games due to his bye week. Also look at upcoming scheduled matchups and playoff matchups.

158 Consider who you are trading and to whom

Will you face your trading partner in an upcoming game? Will your helping him in this trade help him to beat you in a regular season matchup? Will you be likely to face them in the playoffs? Will this trade help them make the playoffs and, if so, at the expense of which other team? Would you rather your trading partner not make the playoffs? All good questions to ask before pulling the trigger on a trade.

159 Buy Low, Sell High

Trade away (sell) players coming off a season high week or if the next stretch of schedule is against them. Trade for (buy) players coming off a tough schedule (they should do better) or who have not performed as expected.

Chapter 10 Miscellaneous Tips

160 Learn everything you can about fantasy football

There are some great books available about fantasy football. My first book, *Fantasy Football Guidebook: Your Comprehensive Guide to Playing Fantasy Football* provides over 400 pages of strategies, tips and theories of fantasy football. It also includes the history of fantasy football and entire chapters on IDP, Auction and Keeper/Dynasty leagues. Refer to Fantasy Football Guidebook for even more tips and draft strategies and for all the analysis behind why these are my favorites.

Other books I highly recommend are David Dorey's *Fantasy Football The Next Level: How to Build a Championship Team Every Season*. David is the co-founder of www.TheHuddle.com and offers a great technique for determining what effect your scoring rules have on positions. League Analysis and Graphing (LAG) is a quick and easy process for visualizing "the unique characteristics of your league". Many of the techniques and concepts mentioned in this book are proven by David's research with LAG. He quotes 25 rules in his book and all are worthy of attention.

What better reference source than "Six of the Worlds Best Fantasy Footballers", that is what *Fantasy Football's Big Six* brings to the table. It truly is as advertised "a fantasy football library in one book." Tapping into areas previously uncovered, Fantasy Football's Big 6 reveals secrets from six of the bigger names in the High Stake Fantasy Football world. Highlighted by Rob Zarzycki (author of Drafting to Win) this 200-page book delves into such topics as IDP leagues, Auction leagues and my favorites, Salary Cap and Draft Masters.

Bob Ashmen makes a convincing argument for Salary Cap leagues as the fairest Fantasy Football contest ever invented. He then goes on to explain some of his money winning strategies. It is a great glimpse into these previously unknown formats. The same goes for Mark Moyer and his examination of Draft Masters. The skills and strategies for these types of leagues are different than your standard redraft leagues and he takes the reader into his war room and reveals all.

Jules "Red Ryder" Mclean excites with her take on Dynasty and Keeper leagues (her forte) and Todd Ullman and Mike Weber finish up with their incredibly gifted advice on Individual Defensive Players and Auctions respectively.

And what of "Z-Man"? Rob covers his area of expertise by exploring redraft leagues and the strategies he has used to win at the World Championship of Fantasy Football (WCOFF). Speaking of winning, these six experts have over half a million ($500,000+) in career Fantasy Football money. Not bad at all for an obsession most of us call a hobby!

No library would be complete without what I consider the first true book on fantasy football, *Drafting to Win: The Ultimate Guide to Playing Fantasy Football* by Robert Zarzycki. Rob's analytical approach to WCOFF and his in depth revelations on how he prepared for a draft opened eyes everywhere. I am impressed with his discussion of "checks and balances" with regards to cheat sheets. "Raise a red flag when you discover…any ranked player is ranked more than fifteen places off by another source".

161 Diversify

Try to have no more than three players from the same team and no more than two starters and not a QB-WR combo. This should be the plan going into the draft. Of course, if you draft Reggie Wayne and Peyton Manning falls to you in the fourth round, I am not saying to pass on him as well. To quote Bill Murray in Ghostbusters, "actually it's more of a guideline than a rule". But if you have a choice between two equal QBs and one is throwing to your stud WR and the other is not, avoid the combo. Same situation, one QB is on the same team as your stud RB, the other is not. Avoid drafting teammates if at all possible.

162 When not to use your overall cheat sheet

Your overall cheat sheet is derived from Value Based Drafting (VBD) (See tip # 96). It is based on a baseline, hopefully the 100-player baseline (See Tip #97). You need to stop using it after all the baselines have been drafted (normally from 100-120 picks into the draft). This occurs somewhere around the 8th round. At this point, your overall cheat sheet is no longer used and your positional cheat sheets will be used to get handcuffs, sleepers, bye week fillers, etc.

Remember to consider team needs when using VBD (your overall cheat sheet). If you only start 2 WRs and you already have 3 WRs, a fourth, although recommended by the cheat sheet, may not be best for your team. Your cheat sheet does not consider bye weeks. If you already have 2 RBs on bye week 6 and VBD suggests a RB on bye week 6 also, consider another RB.

Your overall cheat sheet does not recommend handcuffs, so a decision to handcuff the backup to a key player is your decision. Finally, VBD does not take into account players with good SOS to either offset another player on the team or for the playoffs.

163 Increase your luck - Watch the games

Watch the NFL games on Thursday night, Sunday and Monday nights. Lucky owners make their own luck by being in the right place at the right time; watching the NFL games on Thursday, Sunday and Monday nights and staying up on the news (injuries, benchings, etc.) and then going to the league site and taking advantage of that news. For example, you see stat tracker says Fred Jackson rushes for 66 yards and a TD instead of

Marshawn Lynch. You go to the internet (before the halftime highlights, because then everyone will know what happened) to see how many carries F. Jackson has and see that he has all of the rushes since the 1st quarter and Lynch went out with a broken foot. You then drop a scrub from your bench and add Jackson to use next week or in subsequent weeks. Is that lucky or was that destiny?

Another example involves your RB Lynch again. This time it turns out that he was in an "accident" and will not start. This information comes out 30 minutes before game time. If you have his handcuff in Fred Jackson you can start him, if not at the very least you can start another RB who may score you some points. Either way you are much better off for knowing his status before the game. If you had not been watching the pre-game shows, but instead were out cutting the grass before the game started, you would have lost a starting player's potential points.

Look for little things during the game to give you an insight into if the team is taking a new direction. For example, "if the offense has four receivers on the field, the majority of the time the quarterback will be throwing the football" according to *Football For Dummies*. But if the offense does this consistently, they may have moved to a more pass oriented offensive scheme overall.

164 Do not carry an extra TE, K or defense unless forced

Do not waste roster spots on an extra TE, K, or DEF unless the rules force you to do so. If the rules state that you must carry a certain number of those positions (such as two each) then you have no choice. **If the rules do not state how many of each position you must have on your roster, carry only 1 TE, 1 K and 1 DEF. HINT: Try to draft each of those players so that they all have a different bye week; (i.e. TE has bye on week 7, K on week 8, DEF on week 9); if at all possible, try to get later bye weeks** versus earlier bye weeks. This will give you more time to figure out if they are any good before the bye week and perhaps an add/drop will be better than picking up a fill-in for that position. Why carry only one from each position? It frees up roster spots for sleeper picks in other, more critical, positions. Simply carrying one at all three positions will free up three places for sleepers. When the first of those players has his bye week (TE in week 7, in above example) then you will need to make a decision to either cut the TE and get a better one off the FA list (hopefully who has already had his bye) or drop one of the sleeper picks who has not panned out and pick up a fill-in TE for this week only. TEs, Ks and DEFs with a bye week in week 9 or 10 are like gold if they are good, since they can be drafted and held almost until the playoffs, before needing to make a decision on the sleepers you drafted in the extra spots.

165 Tips change - be flexible

Things change – not all tips will be great (or even apply) 10 years from now. Do not get in a tizzy if one or more of these 201 tips starts to leak a little, given some time. The NFL changes, trends change, rules change and the statistics some of these tips are based on will change. Take it all in stride. If you know the foundations for why these tips are the way they are, and I have tried to explain them in good order. then you can make your own tips and adjust and adapt. Flexibility is the key to fantasy football success.

166 Play the percentages

Know when to take chances and when the odds are not in your favor. If Tony Romo has a 50% chance of a good or great game this week and your other QB (A. Rodgers) has a 30% chance of a good or great game. Why would you choose Rodgers? Play the percentages and go with Romo. Know what to expect and when to expect it. Do not bet on long shots unless you are hedged enough (sleepers on roster but not starting until they prove themselves). Sometimes you have to go against the odds to get a win. If you squeaked into the playoffs and face the top scoring team in the league and are behind by 15 going into the late games, maybe you do need to take some chances versus playing the percentages, but those are exceptional circumstances.

If you are to play the percentages, first identify the various scenarios that can occur. Then assign probabilities to each scenario. If you need help with the probabilities look at message boards or expert columns. These can give you a good feel for what most think will happen and this can translate into a close approximation of the odds. For example, if you think there is a 80% chance of a WR starting this year, a 15% chance of him just filling in for the stud occasionally and a 1% chance that he will be jailed or released, now you have a better way to rank him based on his projections based on the percentages.

167 Use the Keep It Simple Sam (KISS) principle

Most know this as "Keep It Simple Stupid", but I hate to use the word stupid in most contexts so I use Sam. Stay with similar formats to make research easier. If you are in three leagues and they are all the same scoring format that will help the ranking go easier since player A in all three leagues may be about the same. Economy of scale will also help with free agents since your research may discover a gem that is available in multiple leagues or at least can go on all your watch lists.

168 FF Magazines

Rule number one is that they are not current when you purchase them. They are old news since they are sent to the printer in May. You get them in July. Update them for injuries, suspensions, retirements, holdouts, etc. I prefer two reliable long-time publications, *Fantasy Football Index* and *Fantasy Football Pro Forecast*. Both provide exactly what I want as a fantasy footballer. Expert rankings with which to compare my rankings, articles on the progression of fantasy football and team information like coaching changes, player additions, etc. In reality these magazines are hard copies of the data I get from the web (See Tip #169) but I still like the magazines because it gives me something to read on vacation or while reading with my wife; versus being tied to the computer. Look for my own rankings, commentary and mock auction team in Fantasy Football Index magazine.

169 FF websites

There is one I find myself gravitating to each year. FootballGuys (www.fantasyfootballguys.com), which I found recently as an add-on to joining the WCOFF. In other words, you got a subscription to FootballGuys free simply by playing in the World Championship of Fantasy Football. But I digress. The FootballGuys site has tons of articles, player stats, depth charts, a drafting software program known as the draft dominator, daily news emails and a great Sunday injury/starters/weather update area. I am not saying they are the only website to use but simply mentioning one site that I have found to have everything I need. If you do decide to join up with them, tell them I sent you.

Yes, you do need a web site. For the price of $20-25 believe me, they are well worth the cost. You will save so much time in hunting down information that they are worth the cost five times over; if you value your Sundays and do not wish to be tied to a computer frantically looking for starters or injury information. Get a reliable web site and one that sends daily updates via email.

I answer questions at www.Fantasyindex.com in their weekly "Ask the Expert" column. Please feel free to comment there or suggest other questions for the column.

170 Avoid TMTS (Too Many Teams Syndrome)

Why not play in a number of leagues? Because the more leagues you play in, the greater the chance of crossover players. Crossover players are players that hurt you in one league (because your opponent has them) and help in another league because you have started them. I hate the feeling when I see that my starting RB is also playing against me in another league. Now you face the nightmare scenario of wanting F. Gore to be shut down in one league and in another rooting for him to have 3 TDs and 150 yards. There is nothing you can do about this problem except limit the number of leagues you play in. By limiting the number of leagues you play in you can focus all of your attention on those few leagues. That way you can be very competitive in those leagues. And avoid crossover players.

How many leagues are too many? I know most will have a local league that they play in. More will also dabble in one of the online leagues or satellite leagues for the bigger championships. So 2-3 is the most I would recommend playing in. I played in 12 in 2007 and regretted some of them. Then in 2008 I played in 15 leagues and fantasy football felt more like a job than the fun hobby it is supposed to be. And, you know what? I have more fun and enjoy the games more when I am in fewer leagues.

Chapter 11 High Stake Leagues (WCOFF, NFFC, FFPC)

Along with all of the other tips presented here are a few especially for the High Stakes Leagues.

171 Make sure the league has payouts escrowed or is a long running league

Unfortunately, over the past few years there have been some instances of companies running fantasy football leagues and contests but not paying out the prizes at the end of the season. There are two ways to combat this. One is to make sure the entity you are dealing with has their prize money in escrow. I only know of one high stakes league that does this. "The Fantasy Football Players Championship is the first and only fantasy event to place its entire prize pool into a secured Attorney Escrow Account. For Players - By Players LLC will hold all prize monies in this secure Attorney Escrow Account, where they will remain for the duration of the NFL season. At no point during the season will any member of For Players - By Players LLC access these funds. Upon the completion of the season, and once winners have been determined, funds will be disbursed directly to the winning players and the process shall be overseen by our Certified Public Accountant." This is what happened in 2008 and it looks like they will always do this. Good on them!

The other precaution you can take is to play in an event where the sponsor has a good track record of paying out. WCOFF is the biggest high stakes event and they have a seven-year record of paying out their winners. I feel safe playing with the WCOFF. The National Fantasy Football Championship is not as big as WCOFF and only has a five-year track record, but they also have NBC as their corporate sponsor so that gives them some additional fire power. I have played in the WCOFF, NFFC and FFPC and will continue to do so in the future. I believe in the integrity of each of these high stakes contests.

172 Scout your opponents

As soon as the leagues are released and you see your opponents, do a little research. First, search for all their posts on the site's message board. This can give you a great insight into what their thoughts are on various topics. Be careful as sometimes MB posts are just chaff in the wind to distract future opponents. But for the most part, posts are honest evaluations of players and strategies and you may be able to find out a strategy or two that a rival will use and you can put that knowledge to good use. Owner X, who is drafting last (you have 11th next to him), has openly stated that he hates the WR-WR start of a draft. If you are drafting you now can be reasonably sure that one of the two WRs you covet will be available after the turn.

Do not just stop at the MB. Dig deeper; Google them (my editor is having a tizzy now). Do not forget to search for a name both ways: first name, last name and last name, first name. Try it out with me; "Sam Hendricks" and "Hendricks, Sam". Notice all of the blog comments I have made about different strategies, etc. This can be very revealing information. Use it wisely and be careful what you post and tell about your plans too.

173 Get to the draft early

The High Stakes leagues draft live in Las Vegas, NV mainly (WCOFF, FFPC and NFFC) with some offering other venues as well. Dallas, Atlantic City and Orlando are also offered by the WCOFF; while the NFFC has New York and Chicago on another weekend. So, no matter where you want to draft or when, these leagues have you covered. However, get to the draft city early and by early I mean at least a day before the draft. Most drafts are on Saturday morning, so plan to arrive Friday afternoon. There is no worse feeling than being late for your draft. I plan to arrive two days early so I can find the venue where the draft will be held. I also like to get over any jet lag and just settle in and get in my comfort zone. Rushing to check in at your hotel and then running to the draft without any updates on the latest information is a recipe for disaster.

174 Use the Thursday game (WCOFF and FFPC)

Both the WCOFF and FFPC conduct their drafts after the Thursday night Kick Off game, so you will know exactly how those players performed on Thursday. Use this to your advantage (see Tip #27). If some no name backup had a great game, think about grabbing him with a late pick. It would have been a sleeper anyway and this way you can use the player for the first week and get that great performance. If he was just a flash in the pan, then you can dump him and add another sleeper.

175 Clock Management

Sometimes it is smarter to pass your turn. If the rules allow, an owner may pass his pick and his pick is awarded to the next owner. After the subsequent owner picks the turn then reverts back to the passed owner. If this is the case, you can basically let the next owner go before you and then you get your pick. Usually you do not get the full 90 seconds when it comes back to you; only 5 seconds. So be ready if you do pass. But why is it OK to do this? You are just letting the next guy go in front of you. When would this make sense?

Usually this occurs around the corner, when you have a pick and then the next owner has two picks and then it comes back to you. You are the 11th pick in a 12-team league. In round 5, you pass on pick 5.11. Team 12 goes next and picks his draft choice for his 5.12. Then it comes back to you for 5.11. After you make your pick, it will go back to a normal rotation with 6.01 and you picking 6.02. What you have done is force Team 12 to reveal what he is going to do. You can use that to your advantage. You are trying to decide between a RB or a WR. There are two left in tiers on your cheat sheet. But if you go RB and Team 12 goes WR-WR. Then you lose out on your WR. By passing you can see which way he is going. He picks WR. Now you can go with the other WR and know that even if he goes RB with his next pick (6.01) you will still get your RB with 6.02. A complicated but effective strategy if it is allowed by the rules.

176 Play in a Satellite right before the Main Event

There is no better tune up than playing in a smaller version of the main event. A satellite league has the same rules as the main event but is offered via an online draft and for a much lower entry fee. You are only playing for league prizes (not playing for a Grand Prize; although both WCOFF and NFFC have something different beyond league prizes in some cases) and because of this the payouts and hence the ROI (Tip # 16) are higher. A satellite is like a practice for the main event in that you can see which players are drafted where. You can also see how many players are drafted from each position overall. For all of these reasons try to have the satellite draft just before the main event but as close to it as possible. Your data will be much more reliable for the main event if it comes from a recent satellite. The satellite you drafted for in May is probably not a realistic view of what will happen in September.

177 Use the ADP data provided by the real drafts

Many of the high stakes leagues now provide the ADP data from their satellites to participants free of charge. I know in 2008 WCOFF posted theirs on the message board and NFFC made it available through emails. Both ADP sets are different since the formats are slightly different for both championships. The NFFC uses 6 points per passing TD, while WCOFF uses 4 points. NFFC awards only .5 points for a RB reception, while WCOFF awards a full point. These are some of the major differences in scoring. Of course another major difference is the NFFC is a 14-team format, while WCOFF is a 12-team format.

The ADP data from each of these big leagues is invaluable because it reflects what actual owners are doing in real satellite drafts with the exact same scoring rules, rosters, etc. (See Tip #39). Some websites may offer the ADP for these leagues for a price, but be wary of where they get their data. Straight from the horse's mouth is usually pretty reliable versus getting it second hand.

178 Draft is single most important event

The draft is the most important factor in success at WCOFF, NFFC or FFPC. Large rosters (20 players or more; starting ten or less) give you plenty of room to stockpile players. These high stakes leagues are about drafting smart, because the leftovers at the skill positions (after 240 players are gone) are non-existent. Once you have your team, your start/bench decisions will mean the difference between first, second or third place (and no championship game) and your FA bidding can be the extra points that get you into the money of the playoffs.

179 Use draft spot to formulate a plan - guaranteed to know it

You will know your draft spot in advance. Fantasy Football Players Championship (FFPC) announces early draft slots the weekend of the 7-8th of August in 2009. The remaining slots are announced after all entries are closed. Most of the big leagues do the same type of thing. If you enter early enough, you can see your draft slot and start to prepare. That is exactly what you should do. Pay your entry fee just in time to get an early draft spot announcement and then practice drafting from that spot for the next month. Note there is no promise of a better draft slot with the early announcement, just that you will know what your spot is well before the draft. But it could be #1 or #12.

180 KDS strategy

The NFFC uses a KDS (Kentucky Derby Style) system, which allows owners to pick a draft spot preference in advance of the random selection of leagues. NFFC participants get to rank their draft spot preference before leagues are formed. The theory is that some input is better than none. Undoubtedly, many players list spots 1-3 in that order, but after that some may prefer to move down in the draft to secure higher picks around the turn. Still others may prefer a lower pick to the middle, so that they can use predictions on what the owners ahead of them will do so that they can get value. As an example, picks 1-7 will be ranked 1st through 7th but then perhaps 10th and 11th get higher preference than 8th and 9th. The NFFC will use each team's preference within a league to determine draft spots after the order of preferences are determined. So the team that is picked as the first choice gets just that, his first choice on the preference sheet. The next team gets their first choice, unless it was already taken by the first team. In theory the last team with the 14th pick could get a much higher draft spot because other teams did not want that spot. Therefore, KDS should improve an owner's draft position simply by allowing more choice rather than assign a spot based on a random drawing.

Having explained the KDS, now how can you use it to your advantage? Play the system. If you think the top 3 or 4 picks will not be as big as everyone else thinks, go for a middle spot and try to get the better 2nd round pick. If you like "playing the corner" (Tip # 107) put 2,3,12 and 13 as your top choices. Plan a strategy based on where you want to be, draft spot-wise and then look at the MB to see where others are leaning. If a NFFC post on the MB says most are going 1-14, then you can be certain to get the 12th or 13th spot if you want them. Those spots are more valuable due to 3RR too (see Tip # 181).

181 3RR Strategy

What is 3RR? 3RR is third round reversal; where the draft order of the third round reverses from a normal serpentine order to prevent the top half of the draft from getting too much advantage (see Tip #5, 29). Why was it introduced into the NFFC in 2007? In 2005, 43% of the league champions picked in spots 1-3 and it became more pronounced in 2006, as 18 of the Top 32 teams (over 56%) drafted from picks 1-3; thus the decision to try 3RR.

In this case, round 3 will have a reversal so that the first pick in round 3 will be team 14 and then it will go back down to team 1, who will get the last pick in round 3 (unlike a true serpentine draft where team 1 would get the first pick). This is designed to even the playing field a bit. Rounds 4-18 will then be serpentine (round 4 will have team 1 pick first, round 5 will have team 14 pick first, and so on).

The format looks like this:
Round 1 1-14
Round 2 14-1
Round 3 14-1
Round 4 1-14
Round 5 14-1
Round 6 1-14

And so on, doubling back every round from here on out, through round 18.
So, having draft spots in the last half of the draft is not so bad, since you get picks first in the 2nd and 3rd rounds.

182 WCOFF tip

Wait on drafting a TE. They make terrible flex players and you can get a serviceable TE in the middle rounds. Get one of the top 10 TEs but do not waste a 4th rounder on one of the top ones.

If anything, a late 4th or early 5th pick on a top 5 TE may be worth it.

One extra bonus WCOFF tip and this one saves you $100 on the entrance fee. **If you play in WCOFF for the first time and use code "slam" you get $100 off the entrance fee**. It does not get much better than that.

183 NFFC tip

QBs are worth more in these leagues as they score 6 points per passing TDs. So their rankings need to be slightly higher in terms of VBD. Sure, all the QBs get the extra bump in passing TD points, but not all the QBs throw the same amount of TD passes. The top 10 or 12 QBs throw the most TDs and thus have an extra premium attached to them.

184 FFPC tip

TEs can really score well with the 1.5 points per pass reception. They make a good flex option if you have two good TEs. So if you can get value in the middle rounds break with conventional thinking and target a TE2.

Another good tip is to look at WRs and RBs who also return kickoffs or punts. Thanks to the active scoring rule in FFPC these players score with KO/PR TDs. DeSean Jackson, WR for the Eagles, is one such player. Rank these players a little higher because they get a chance at extra TDs from returns.

185 Use the other draft boards from the night before

If you are in Las Vegas anyway, stroll down to the venue and look at some of the other draft boards from the auction drafts, draft masters or big money leagues. Put it all in perspective, though. Make sure you know the rules for each, to make sure it is an apples to apples comparison. Remember that the draft masters is a no free-agency, draft and forget league, so backups are more important then stockpiling in some cases. Use the auction values as a gauge for where a player ranks within his position and overall. If WR A was worth $25 and WR B $30 and RB C $28; you know which was overall higher and where the WRs ranked among themselves. Again remember these values are what one owner thought they were worth but it is a good quick check of your cheat sheets. Use the draft master board with the deep rosters for sleeper research. The big money leagues (or whatever they are called these days) are usually a good bench mark since those teams plunked down over $5,000 or more to play fantasy football. I sit up and listen when those drafts are occurring.

186 Relax

Enjoy it, as it may be a once in a lifetime event. Look around, soak up the ambiance, make some new friends and have a good time. I think the best part is putting a face to the names or call signs on the message boards. You will find that most are like you and share a love for fantasy football, and that is the ultimate bond. Do not get so nervous that you forget to enjoy the event.

187 Have 4-5 players ready to pick in advance

Prepare, prepare, prepare. There is nothing worse than drafting at a high stakes table and announcing that you want a player but then find out he was drafted two rounds ago. Be ready with 4 to 5 players and track who is available and who is not. Do not get distracted by the alcohol, women or other owners. Play your game until the draft is over. Then become distracted by the alcohol, women and other owners.

188 No trades, so stockpile

None of the high stakes leagues allows trades (for good reasons) so stockpile the RB and WR positions. Minimize the K and Defenses and play lots of sleepers on the RB and WR side. I will say it again: you start 6 total RB/WRs a week (2 RBs, 3 WRs and 1 Flex or 2 RBs, 2 WRs and 2 Flex in FFPC) so you better have a ton of good ones.

189 Key to all is PPR

Remember the key is pass receptions! The more passes a player catches, the more points your team earns (1 PPR). More touches also means more chances at TDs and yards. RBs with lots of catches are a gold mine (think Matt Forte). RBs that catch many passes out of the backfield can be serviceable late round additions.

190 Focus on WR

WCOFF and NFFC scoring (PPR combined with requiring 3 WRs to start and having a flex position) does a great job of elevating WRs value relative to RBs. WRs are more important because with three good RBs you can expect each to have a bye week and one game out with injury. That means starting a 4th WR as a flex player for 6 weeks, or almost half of the regular season. Plan on starting a 4th WR as a strategy, and if you have three good RBs some weeks, you are that much better off. In 2008 there was a drop-off between the Top 12 WRs and the other WRs. Another drop-off occurred after the Top 22. Get your WRs early and often; 7-9 WRs are a must. Try to get 2 WRs in the first 4 rounds and then 6 more in rounds 5-17.

191 Consider WR-WR if 11th or 12th pick in WCOFF or FFPC

If you have the 11th or 12th pick, consider WR-WR. You will have to go RB with the 3rd and 4th picks, but you are going against the flow and can find lots of value. It is tough to win a league without one of the stud RBs, but will a good enough RB fall to 11th? Why not take two Top WRs? Statistically the 11th draft spot has done better than the other bottom spots. Perhaps that is because of this strategy.

192 Draft for success - Winning teams average 140 points per week

In a 1 point per 10 yards rushing/receiving, 1 PPR league, 140 points is a winning average. Practice different draft strategies to determine if you can draft a team that scores 140 points a week. If not, perhaps you will need to try a different strategy. There is no reason to draft a mediocre team. You know your draft spot, you know the rules and how to take advantage of them and you know what type of team you need to win. Now figure out how to draft that team.

193 Roster optimization - 2 QBs, 7 RBs, 8 WRs, 1 TE, 1 K and 1 Def

In WCOFF and FFPC your roster consists of 20 players. In most of the cases the above roster is optimized for giving you the best chance of winning. In the FFPC, 2 QBs, 7 RBs, 7 WRs, 2 TEs, 1 K and 1 Def is more likely. In the NFFC you are only allowed 18 players and QBs play more of a role. In NFFC use either 2-3 QBs, 6 RBs, 6-7 WRs, 1 TE, 1 K and 1 Def. In all the leagues this is a rough guide to your normal weighting of positions. A gift on the waiver wire will change these optimizations. By the same token, when the free agency deadline approaches, 2 TEs and 2 Ks are a better lineup. See Tip #131 concerning the single TE, K and Defense.

194 Suggest 1 TE, K and Def but watch bye weeks of them

In order to stockpile more RBs and WRs on your roster, you need to limit the number of TEs, Ks and Defenses to one. If you do this and only have one of these positions, make sure they are on differing bye weeks. The later the bye week the better and best not to have them all on the same bye week; if two of them have the same bye that will mean dropping two sleepers to pick up bye week replacements. Better to have them on bye week 8, 9 and 10. That way you only have to drop one sleeper in week 8 and then can drop the additional player in week 9 for the other bye week replacement. The later the bye week, the easier it will be to cut the sleeper due to non-performance and perhaps even the TE, K or Defenses can be dropped instead if they are not performing.

195 Draft Kicker next to last

Wait on a kicker till after the 12th round and close to the end. If other teams are waiting then grab your K1 after the 12th if you can get the one you want (and he has a late bye week). Usually the 5th or 6th ranked kicker can be had 3 rounds after the first kicker went (so 6th K in the 15th round). Only draft one kicker and use the other spot for your sleeper. You cannot predict Top 5 kickers. The difference between the 5th and 11th kickers, in 2008, was a mere 7.6 points. The 4th and the 16th kicker were separated by 14 points. That is less than 1 point per game, where teams typically score 120 in a week and you want to score 140.

196 Draft Defense late

Wait on defenses too. Many owners rank defenses differently. I have found that simply by waiting (letting five defenses be drafted before you get concerned), I can get one of my Top 10 defenses very late in the draft. Only draft 1 defense and save a spot for a sleeper. Play matchups with the waiver wire until bye weeks are over and you need to get your team ready for a playoff push. The 2008 difference between the 6th and 12th defense was 16 points. Again, this is 1 point per game in a league where teams average 120 a week. The 7th and 11th defense were only off by 4 points. Why rush to get mediocrity?

197 Have a co-manager

Share duties with a co-manager. Why? Split costs, help with draft day tracking and great to have a sounding board for decisions. This can help you with the workload and ease the transition into a new league or system. Perhaps after co-managing one year, you can then go it on your own the following year. Be careful of co-managing though, since these arrangements can cause disagreements and damage to friendships. Know the other owner and have definite guidelines for who does what; what the other owner can do independently and what they both must do together. Who sets the lineup? Who can authorize a trade? Do both have website access? Who pays what costs? Drafting duties? Best if one can focus on drafting and cheat sheets while other tracks other owners' tendencies and predicts whom the other owners will take in picks leading up to yours. Oh yeah, he/she can be a great wingman when you go celebrate after the draft.

198 Use a loyalty discount to lower cost of entry

Many of the high stakes leagues are offering "loyalty discounts" to players from the previous year. If you played in the main event the year prior and sign up early you get a discount off the normal entry fee. This is a great tool to lower your cost and increase your return on investment. If it costs $1300 to play but you can enter for $1275, then you have just increased your ROI when you win! Another bonus is the second entry discount. Some leagues allow you to play a second team at a reduced price. For example, FFPC is offering a second team for $1200 ($100 off their normal price of $1300). So two teams for $2475...

Again another reminder, if you are going to play WCOFF for the first time this year. Use code "slam" to get $100 off the entrance fee.

199 Decide if you are playing for money or fame, or both

Some leagues allow multiple teams. See Tip #198. I personally do not like this option. I prefer to play in leagues where it is one man, one team, one chance. Sure, I can co-manage a number of other teams with other owners but the only winner should be the primary owner. I like leagues with one owner as the primary winner and the co-owner as a care-taker. Only one owner gets the glory, trophy and the money.

Let us say Bill Gates wants to win the FFPC in 2009. I get in first with www.FFGuidebook.com, shamelessly promoting my book, and then Bill buys the remaining 299 teams. He names them creatively Bill Gates 1-299. He cannot draft for all 299 simultaneously so he hires a firm to provide 298 "co- managers" who draft for him and manage the day-to-day operations of those other teams. However, the listed owner is Bill Gates for all of them. I agree he has invested much more than I. Thus when he wins his ROI will be crap. However, his chances of winning are much higher than mine simply because he has so many more teams. "Quantity has a quality all its own." (Napoleon)

Surprise, team Bill Gates 69 wins the FFPC. Who is named the winner? You guessed it, BILL GATES. Not his great co-owner who got him the win. All of the media report that Bill Gates won the FFPC. Now in my opinion Bill Gates winning the FFPC in this scenario lessens the achievement of winning this prestigious event. I have taken multiple teams to the ultimate extreme but at what point do you draw a line in the sand? Are two teams okay, but not five? What about 10? 30? 50? I do not have a good answer. All I know is that by keeping it to one team-one person-one chance, it is easy to say "everyone has one chance of winning."

We play this great hobby for many reasons. One of which is the monetary aspect (always good to win some cash since if you win more than you spend it is a sign of greatness). Nevertheless, another reason is the "Glory" of being the best in an event for that year; you know the "Best of the best." If a person has multiple chances to win simply because they can buy more teams, than that does not seem fair to me. I realize the FFPC and WCOFF and NFFC want to have more teams so they can provide more prizes and make more money at the same time. I think more teams are fine but allowing multiple teams per person cheapens the achievement in some way.

200 Do not drop unproductive sleepers too early

Do not drop unproductive players too early (especially RBs). Let them flail at least until week 6 before you drop them. Injuries to them are a different rule. This just applies to performance (although all too often an injury usually is the cause for the poor performance). In general, it is better to hold a player a little too long than to drop them too early and miss the return to productivity. Four to five games is a good indicator of what they will do for the season. But also factor in who they played during these early games. Sleepers are good picks, but if dropped too early someone else gets the benefit of their breakout, while all you did was waste a draft spot on them, initially. Dominik Hixon and, to a limited extent, Deuce McCallister in 2008 fit this mold. Hixon had a great preseason but then failed to start until P. Buress had his off field problems. Deuce was slow to return from his injury.

201 Do not spend your entire Sunday involved in Fantasy Football

Take a break from the hobby every now and then. The time off will make you appreciate fantasy football even more and it may just save your marriage.

202 Never play in the same league as Sam "Slam" Hendricks (an extra tip in case I miscounted or had same one twice)

This is a simple one. Some leagues let you see who is in them before you decide to sign up. It does not happen often and in my opinion should never be done but it does occur on occasion, particularly in satellite leagues of some of the aforementioned High Stake Leagues. Many times it happens through message board posts, where a thread is started by others who have joined early, before it fills up. If you are thinking of joining one of these leagues and you see any of the more well-known fantasy footballers (for example Rob Zarzycki, Dave Gerczak (2008 NFFC Champion), Alex Kaganovsky, Louis Tranquilli, Jules McLean, Todd Ullman, Billy Waz or myself) do not sign up for that league. Realistically you are playing against a tougher opponent than if you joined a similar league without one of the better fantasy footballers out there. In NFL terms, who would you rather play? The Detroit Lions or the Indianapolis Colts? Of course, if you want to play against the best, be my guest.

The corollary is to scout out any players you know are in that league. Sometimes they will reveal this information on the league or contest's message board (MB). If you know who is in league 17 and it has three slots open, research who your competition will be if you join. If it turns out that four of the nine players already signed up are League Champions from last year and finished in the top ten the past two years, then I say pass on that stiff competition. Why join a league overloaded with great competition? Instead find one, if possible, with lots of new owners who may have some new league jitters and just may make a mistake or two.

If you join a league and then find out there are lots of veterans, don't panic. Just research them and see if you can find some weaknesses. Read their articles or book if they have one published. Find out what they like to do. Perhaps they like to wait on QBs (a good strategy that I propose in Tip # 71). Perhaps you can take advantage of that by snatching your 2nd QB before them and in the process steal who they were waiting on. Or use their own rankings against them (modified of course).

Appendix A Draft Tracker
(12 Teams, 20 Player Roster)

Pos/Team	1	2	3	4	5	6	7	8	9	10	11	12
QB1												
QB2												
RB1												
RB2												
RB3												
RB4												
RB5												
RB6												
RB7												
WR1												
WR2												
WR3												
WR4												
WR5												
WR6												
TE1												
TE2												
K1												
K2												
DEF1												
DEF2												

Appendix B Supply and Demand Table

Pos	NFL	FF Players (4)	8 Team	10 Team	12 Team	14 Team	16 Team
QB	32	2	16(50%)	20(63%)	24(75%)	28(88%)	32(100%)
RB	36 (1)	3 4	24(67%) 32(89%)	30(94%) 40(120%	36(100%) 48(133%)	42(117%) 56(156%)	48(133%) 64(178%)
WR	70 (2)	4 5	32(46%) 40(57%)	40(57%) 50(71%)	48(69%) 60(86%)	56(80%) 70(100%)	64(91%) 80(114%)
TE	32	2	16(50%)	20(63%)	24(75%)	28(88%)	32(100%)
K	32	2	16(50%)	20(63%)	24(75%)	28(88%)	32(100%)
DEF	32	2	16(50%)	20(63%)	24(75%)	28(88%)	32(100%)
DL	124 (3)	4	32(26%)	40(32%)	48(39%)	56(45%)	64(52%)
LB	100 (3)	5	40(40%)	50(50%)	60(60%)	70(70%)	80(80%)
DB	128	4	32(25%)	40(31%)	48(37%)	56(44%)	64(50%)

Notes:
1) 1 primary RB per team plus 4 RBBC teams
2) 2 WRs per team plus 6 WR3's who are good enough to start
3) Based on teams using 3-4 and 4-3
4) 2 RBs +3 WRs as starters plus a backup at each position is the top number. The bottom number is based on leagues with 2 RBs +3 WRs, and 1 Flex position and one backup.

Appendix C Cheat Sheet Sample-QB

Adj	Rank	Player Name	Team	Bye	Notes	ADP
	1	Peyton Manning	IND	6	Lost OC	3.03
Up	2	Drew Brees	NO	5	No RB	2.12
	3	Aaron Rodgers	GB	5		3.11
?	4	Tom Brady	NE	8	Inj 08'	3.02
		End Tier 1				
++	5	Kurt Warner	AZ	4	Age?	4.02
Up	6	Donovan McNabb	PHI	4	New WR	4.12
	7	Phillip Rivers	SD	5		5.05
Up	8	Tony Romo	DAL	6	Lost T.O	5.07
		End Tier 2				
Dn	9	Jay Cutler	CHI	5	New tm	6.04

About the Author

Sam "Slam" Hendricks was born and raised in Lynchburg, Virginia and graduated from the University of Virginia in 1986. He joined the USAF and flew RF4C fighter jets in Germany during the Cold War. He transitioned into the F15E Strike Eagle and earned three aerial achievement medals during combat missions in Operation Desert Storm.

He left the Air Force in 1993 to work for McDonnell Douglas as an F15E instructor, a job he has performed for more than 16 years. Sam spent the last ten years in the Middle East and Europe. He and his Danish wife, Birgitte, recently moved to Virginia and now live in the foothills of the Blue Ridge Mountains.

He participates in the World Championship of Fantasy Football (WCOFF), National Fantasy Football Championship (NFFC) and the Fantasy Football Players Championship (FFPC). He has won numerous league championships in his 19-year fantasy football career. He is a member of the Fantasy Sports Writers Association (FSWA).

He has a MBA in Business and a Masters in Personal Finance. His next book (release date May 2010) will be on personal finance and the day-to-day things we can all do to improve our finances.

LaVergne, TN USA
18 February 2011
217136LV00002B/48/P